WOMEN AGAINST
VIOLENCE
BREAKING THE SILENCE

Reflecting on Experience in
Latin America and the Caribbean

Edited by ANA MARIA BRASILEIRO

United Nations Development Fund
for Women (UNIFEM)
New York, USA

The United Nations Development Fund for Women (UNIFEM) was created as a result of the energetic advocacy of women at the 1975 International Women's Year (IWY) Tribune in Mexico City. Established by the United Nations in 1976 as the Voluntary Fund for the UN Decade for Women, UNIFEM became an autonomous organization within the UN family in 1985. UNIFEM's mission is to promote the economic and political empowerment of women in developing countries. UNIFEM works to ensure the participation of women in all levels of development planning and practice. UNIFEM also acts as a catalyst within the UN system for efforts to link the needs and concerns of women to all critical issues on the national, regional and global agenda. This collection of articles is the fourth of a four-part series that reflects on UNIFEM's experience with projects and programmes in Latin America and the Caribbean.

The views expressed in this book are those of the authors and do not necessarily represent the views of UNIFEM, the United Nations or any of its affiliated organizations.

Women' Against Violence: Breaking the Silence
Edited by Ana Maria Brasileiro
ISBN 0-912917-32-6
Series Title: Reflecting on Experience

© 1997 The United Nations Development Fund for Women

United Nations Development Fund for Women
304 East 45th Street, 6th Floor, New York, NY 10017 USA
Phone: (212) 906-6400 Fax: (212) 906-6705
E-mail: unifem@undp.org
Internet: http://www.unifem.undp.org

All UNIFEM publications are distributed by Women, Ink.
777 UN Plaza, 3rd Floor, New York, NY 10017 USA
Phone: (212) 687-8633 Fax: (212) 661-2704

SPONSORED BY THE GOVERNMENT OF JAPAN

Cover & book design: a. piccolo graphics
Cover photo: Joan Roth

Contents

Preface 1
Virginia Vargas

Introduction: Violence Against Women 5
Roxanna Carrillo

Violence Against Women: A Regional Crisis 16
Marcela Ortiz

Women's Human Rights and Latin American Criminal Law 28
Gladys Acosta Vargas

Combatting Violence Against Women in the Caribbean 51
Roberta Clarke

Unequal Status, Unequal Development:
   Gender Violence in Mexico 63
Patricia Duarte Sánchez and Gerardo González

The Power Axis:
   A Hierarchy of Violence in Brazil 74
Heleith I. B. Saffioti

Beyond the Conventions:
   Violence Prevention in the Andean Region 87
Alexandra Ayala Marín

Taking Action Against Violence:
   A Case Study in Trinidad and Tobago 100
Cecilia Babb

Notes on Contributors 115

"Violence against women is pervasive not just in war or refugee camps but on the street, in the workplace, and in the home. Domestic violence not only causes physical suffering but disrupts women's lives and blocks their individual growth and participation in society...

One cannot ignore another kind of violence against women—from which the first derives—the violence of economic systems that do not value the contributions women make."

—Noeleen Heyzer, World Summit for Social Development,
Copenhagen, March 1995

Acknowledgements

This book represents more than the thinking and experience of the women whose names are listed as contributors. It is a reflection of over two decades of work by thousands of women in Latin America and the Caribbean who have refused to be silent in the face of violence against women. These women, too numerous to name, have spoken out against gender-based violence and taken action to combat it. Because of them, gender-based violence, once a private affair, is recognized as a public responsibility, and a major obstacle to development.

The voices and experiences of women activists, advocates and academics in countries and communities worldwide come to us at the UNIFEM headquarters in New York through our network of Regional Programme Advisors (RPAs). The articles in this book and the inspiration for pulling them together, could not have happened without in-depth consultation with Guadalupe Espinosa in Mexico, Joycelin Massiah in Barbados, Branca Moreira Alves in Brazil, and Monica Munoz in Ecuador. Guadalupe Espinosa in our Mexico office and Karen Judd at headquarters took responsibility for editing the manuscripts and moving the production process along. Claudine Correia, Programme Officer in the Latin American/Caribbean section at UNIFEM, and Ana Cecilia Quintanilla, who has backstopped so many efforts for this section, were also valuable and committed partners in this effort.

Finally, we need to acknowledge our colleagues at UNIFEM, who are tireless in their efforts to advocate and raise funds for women's efforts worldwide. It is the collective effort of all UNIFEM staff that keeps the infrastructure for supporting women's organizing and empowerment alive.

—*Ana Maria Brasileiro*

Preface

VIRGINIA VARGAS

Resistance and struggle against the violence that society exercises against women, of all classes and racial backgrounds, represents one of the most powerful and active currents within the modern feminist movement. The Latin-Caribbean region's first feminist calendar date—25 November—is also its first contribution to the global women's movement: "25 November, No More Violence Against Women Day," named in honour of "las Mariposas," three sisters in the Dominican Republic killed on that date in 1960 for their refusal to be intimidated by the dictatorship, is now recognized by women, civil society, and in many cases, governments, throughout the region. Regional networks focussing on violence and women's human rights—especially ISIS International and the Latin American Committee for the Defense of Women's Rights (CLADEM)—as well as those that deal with the dynamics of inclusion and exclusion in our societies, have incorporated positions against all types of violence against women within their work. It is around this complex and dramatic aspect of women's lives, therefore, that the feminist movement has come together, within civil society, the state, and international institutions, impelled by the urgent need to live in a world that is less hostile towards women.

The struggle against violence against women also brings together the various objectives and strategies of the feminist movement in the region, which have developed along different paths over the years. In the years since its beginning, over 20 years ago, the movement has accumulated a wealth of experience in uncovering the scope and impact of violence in women's lives, in so doing expanding the way in which the feminist movement looks at itself as well as making visible one of the most flagrant aspects of women's subordination, one which most frequently goes unpunished. Women's groups set up shelters and halfway houses for battered and sexually abused women which in turn opened new areas of work and reflection for feminists.   ❖

I

Reflection and experience were nurtured by both pain and uncertainty; rejecting the impunity surrounding violence against women and seeking to transform the tragedy of personal violence into an affirmative public position, activists proposed alternatives that could help all women. It was evident that there was an important next step, one that the women's movement could not take by itself: states and public authorities would have to take on the responsibility for guaranteeing women's well-being and security. Thus local and national authorities as well as judicial bodies would have to enact laws and mechanisms to correct judicial bias and create safe spaces for women to denounce the violence against them. Concrete spaces within the state bureaucracy, such as the Women's Commissaries, have been created in various countries. While this is a good start, it remains to be seen if such expressions of "public conscience" will be effective, or whether the state will have to take stronger enforcement measures. In any case, it is clear that nothing by itself will be effective; a broader and more integrated strategic vision is necessary.

All of this is being made visible at a global level by the initiatives of international agencies and organizations as well as by the international women's movement, which has become a force at the global level, marking a new stage in human rights for women. Governments must respond not only to the pressure of national women's movements but also to their own international commitments, specifically the 1993 Vienna Declaration and the 1994 Inter-American Convention to Prevent, Sanction and Eradicate Violence Against Women, known as the Belem Convention, which have been signed but still not ratified by many governments in the region.

Clearly, the 1993 World Conference on Human Rights in Vienna was the "touchstone," since it laid the basis for this integrated strategic perspective, recognizing women's rights as human rights. The Fourth World Women's Conference and NGO Forum in 1995 consolidated this framework, making explicit the responsibilities of states to ensure women's right to a violence-free life and building a legal and social framework of normative expectations and obligations.

In addition to legislation and government support services, the feminist movement has also begun to search for effective ways to gain acceptance of its expanded world-view. This world-view is based on the recognition, both depressing and encouraging, that it is not possible to deal with violence against women without challenging the basis of the political, economic, socio-cultural and sexual organization of society, that ultimately, violence continues to happen because it is sustained in the myriad expressions of discrimination and subordination and humiliation of women, of every age, every class and all racial groups.

This expanded world-view also enlarges the feminist political position, which insists that confronting violence against women is fundamental to the struggle for democracy and to extend the boundaries of female citizenship in the region. Only by incorporating the struggle against violence can the movement extend democracy in this way, since violence is the thread that links all forms of discrimination against and subordination of women. Democracy in the public and the private sphere; democracy in the home and in the bed as well as in the country; democracy that questions and seeks alternatives to poverty, ignorance and the lack of knowledge and self-esteem that prevent women from taking control of their lives and circumstances; democracy that recognizes the body as basic to the self, the foundation of the emotional persona, our form of relation and affirmation towards life and towards other people. And that at the same time it cannot continue to be a space of power and domination of one sex over another.

In this context, the drama of violence begins to become affirmative, and can transform itself as a defence of women's human rights, as envisioned by women in at the World Conference on Human Rights in Vienna. And this struggle doesn't generate pity, but affirms human rights, propelling a political force capable of making the alliances needed both in the short term, to stop violence against women, and in the long term, to win the recognition that the violence embedded in racist, sexist, homophobic, economic and political discrimination can be challenged and changed by both women and men alike.   ❖

Introduction:
Violence Against Women

ROXANNA CARRILLO

"The human security of women, and the well-being of their dependents, will rely in large measure on the recognition that societies can alter traditions without sacrificing their identity or stability. It will hinge on the ability of religious and cultural communities to emphasize the core values of love and justice over the patriarchal traditions of the subjugation of women. And it will depend on the incorporation of those values into the legal frameworks of national and international bodies."

Almost 50 years ago, in the aftermath of World War II, governments from all continents came together to draft a document that would have a profound impact on the lives of all human beings. The document, known as the Universal Declaration of Human Rights (UDHR), contains a set of basic principles which constitute the fundamental rights and freedoms of every person for the simple fact of having being born human. The Declaration states in unequivocal terms the universal nature of these standards in that they apply to everyone "without distinction of any kind, such as race, colour, sex, language, religion, political or other opinion, national or social origin, property, birth or other status."

Since 1948 other international instruments have further elaborated the principles contained in the UDHR. However, when it comes to the application of these principles with regard to women, governments, as well as the bodies charged with the protection and promotion of human rights, have shown a remarkable myopia. Yet the principles contained in the UDHR have provided individuals, groups and social movements with a powerful ethical vision to anchor their claims for justice.

This article incorporates ideas developed in Charlotte Bunch, Roxanna Carrillo and Rima Shore, "Gender-Based Violence: A Critical Development Issue," in UNDP, Human Development Report 1995 *(New York: Oxford University Press, 1955).*

When the global community convened in Vienna in 1993 for the World Conference on Human Rights, women's-rights advocates utilized this opportunity to put their concerns on the conference agenda. Worldwide mobilization for this goal was led by a coalition of groups from around the world which rallied together in the Global Campaign for Women's Human Rights. Among the several achievements of the Global Campaign was the inclusion of a simple yet profound statement in the Vienna Declaration and Programme of Action: that the human rights of women are an inalienable, integral and indivisible part of universal human rights, that the full participation of women in political, social and cultural life, as well as the eradication of all forms of discrimination on the grounds of sex are priority objectives of the international community, and that gender-based violence and all forms of sexual harassment and exploitation (...) must be eliminated.[1]

Over the last two decades, the issue of violence against women has galvanized organization and mobilization by women from every region, regardless of race, class, ethnicity, ideology, religion or social status. The reality and threat of violence looms over women's everyday lives, coloring their ability to participate in development projects, to exercise democracy, and to engage fully in society. The experience and fear of violence is a consistent thread in women's lives, intertwined with their most basic security needs: personal, community, environmental, economic and political. It limits women's choices directly by destroying their health, disrupting their lives, and constricting the scope of their activity; and indirectly by eroding their self-confidence and self-esteem. In virtually every nation, violence or the threat of it shrinks the range of choices open to women and girls, limiting not only their mobility and their control over their lives, but ultimately also their ability to imagine mobility and control over their lives. Violence against women thus presents a steep barrier to the cultivation of respect for human rights and the achievement of sustainable human development.

Violence Against Women: The International Context

Understanding of the issue of violence against women has improved dramatically in the last 25 years. In 1975, at the UN International Women's Year Conference in Mexico City, violence against women was considered very much a family matter: policy recommendations emphasized the benefits of family counselling and the need for more responsive family courts. As the international women's movement gathered strength, understanding and public awareness gained both force and complexity. At the Second World Conference on Women in Copenhagen in 1980 and five years later at Nairobi, domestic violence was recognized as an obstacle to equality and an intolerable offence to human dignity. In 1985, the UN General Assembly passed its first resolution on violence against women, calling for concerted and multi-disciplinary action to combat domestic violence in all nations.

A few years later, the Committee which oversees the implementation of the Convention on the Elimination of all forms of Discrimination Against Women (CEDAW) issued a recommendation extending the scope of discrimination to include gender-based violence, omitted in the 1979 original text. And in 1993, the General Assembly adopted the Declaration on the Elimination of Violence against Women, further defining this phenomenon and recommending measures to combat it. This was a landmark document in three ways:

- *It situated violence against women squarely within the discourse on human rights,* affirming that women are entitled to equal enjoyment and protection of all human rights and fundamental freedoms, including liberty and security of person, and freedom from torture or other cruel, inhuman or degrading treatment or punishment;
- *It enlarged the concept of violence against women to reflect the real conditions of women's lives,* recognizing not only physical, sexual and psychological violence but also threats of such harm; it addressed violence against women within the family setting as well as within the community, and confronted the issue of violence perpetrated and condoned by the state;
- *It pointed to the gender-based roots of violence,* reflecting the fact that gender-based violence is not random violence in which the victims happen to be women and girls; the risk factor is being female.

According to the Declaration, violence against women encompasses but is not limited to:

- Physical, sexual, and psychological violence occurring in the family, including battering, sexual abuse of female children, dowry-related violence, marital rape, female

genital mutilation and other traditional practices harmful
to women, non-spousal violence and violence related to
exploitation;
• Physical, sexual, and psychological violence occurring
within the community, including rape, sexual abuse,
sexual harassment and intimidation at work, in
educational institutions and elsewhere, trafficking in
women and forced prostitution;
• Physical, sexual and psychological violence perpetrated
or condoned by the state wherever it occurs.

Other forms of violence include violations of the rights of women in
situations of armed conflict, in particular murder, systematic rape, sexual
slavery and forced pregnancy, forced sterilization and forced abortion,
coercive use of contraceptives, female infanticide and prenatal sex-selection.

Organizing Against Gender-Based Violence

Efforts to organize around gender-based violence crystallized around
the UN conferences in the 1990s, particularly the 1993 World Conference
on Human Rights in Vienna, the 1994 International Conference on
Population and Development in Cairo, and the 1995 Fourth World
Conference on Women in Beijing. In Vienna, women's rights advocates
succeeded in getting the recognition by the international community that
violence against women, whether it occurs in public or in private, is a
violation of women's fundamental human rights. The Conference also
called on the Commission on Human Rights to appoint a Special
Rapporteur on violence against women, which it did the following year,
framing the mandate in the language provided by the Declaration on the
Elimination of Violence Against Women.

In Cairo, women introduced the issue of violence as a form of control
of women's health and sexuality and as a clear obstacle to women's right to
self-determination in matters related to their reproduction. In Beijing,
gender-based violence again concentrated much of women's advocacy
efforts, emerging as one of the cornerstones in the implementation of the
agenda for empowerment. As stated in the Platform for Action: "Violence
against women is a manifestation of the historically unequal power relations
between men and women, which have led to domination over and
discrimination against women by men and to the prevention of women's
full advancement."

In spite of these advances, violence against women continues in every region. It is still very difficult to measure the extent of the phenomenon owing to serious problems of data collection. In virtually every country, crime statistics grossly under-report incidences of gender-based violence, particularly in the family setting. However, research conducted in both the global North and the global South indicates that gender-based violence:

- affects females throughout the life-cycle: It can extend from pre-birth and infancy (sex-selected abortion and infanticide) through old age (violence against widows and elder abuse);
- affects women of every nation, belief, class, race and ethnic group. While the discovery of communities where gender-based violence is minimal indicates that it is not inevitable, cross-cultural research indicates that these are the rare exceptions rather than the rule. On the whole, the data supports the conclusion that violence or the threat of violence affects almost all women.
- is exacerbated by poverty, but will not be eliminated through economic remedies alone. Violence against women appears to be associated with poverty and related stress; some studies suggest that wife abuse, for example, is more prevalent among the poor and unemployed. But evidence from the industrialized world indicates that many women in relatively secure economic circumstances cannot extricate themselves from abusive situations. In many cases, their income, social status, child custody rights and self-esteem depend on their continuing to co-habit with their abusers.

Recent cross-cultural studies on family violence and rape, based on data from 90 societies worldwide, suggest that four factors together are strong predictors of the prevalence of violence against women in a society: economic inequality between men and women; a pattern of using physical violence to resolve conflict; male authority and control of decision-making; and restrictions on women's ability to leave the family setting. While these factors may seem self-evident, they are often obscured by the prevalence of several myths about violence against women: that lording power over women is an inherent part of "maleness" and an acceptable exercise of male prerogative; that violence against women has the salutary effect of relieving male tension during periods of stress; that it reflects a natural male tendency to sexual aggression; that it reflects women's inferiority and their desire for men to dominate them; that it is an inevitable and permanent feature of male-female relations.

By contrast, the experience of those working to combat gender violence has demonstrated that violence against women is a function of socially constructed norms of acceptable behaviour, which can be reduced and eliminated only through fundamental changes in the status of women and attitudes towards men and women in society. Such far-reaching social change requires formal and informal education, effective use of media, and a clear commitment from governments not only to enact laws making such practices illegal and subject to punishment, but even more importantly to ensure that the legislation is enforced. The Beijing Platform for Action considers this "a challenging task [but one that is] necessary and achievable," and calls for developing a holistic and multidisciplinary approach to promoting families, communities and states that are free of violence against women.

Key Challenges for the Elimination of Gender-Based Violence

Confronting gender-based violence raises certain problems that set it apart from other kinds of human-rights abuse. For example, when the perpetrator of violence is an outsider, community support usually can be mobilized to fight it. But how can people be persuaded to stop accepting or condoning violence committed by friends and relatives? Further, many human-rights abuses are amenable to legal remedies within the present structures of the law. But the law is not a neutral force in patriarchal societies. How can power holders be motivated to acknowledge, and ultimately relinquish, their own stake in practices that reinforce male control?

These questions point to three key challenges that should inform the policies and practice of women's movements—and the agencies that support them: to find ways to deconstruct traditional power structures and cultural assumptions that sustain continuing gender-based violence; to bring pressure on both the state and community to assume responsibility for eliminating gender-based violence and to hold them accountable if they do not; and to ensure that programmes aimed at promoting sustainable human development include a gender dimension as a critical feature in its formulation, design and implementation.

Running through all of these is the question: What does it take to make local communities and national governments decide that it is their responsibility to prevent such violence? This requires a profound shift in people's attitudes, away from individual blame towards holding an entire community accountable for gender-based violence. Significant change will occur only when the community is seen as responsible for the violence that it has promoted or tolerated by failing to intervene. That approach has been successfully promoted in zero-tolerance campaigns, such as the one that took place in Scotland a few years ago.

A critical element in any strategy to eliminate violence against women is a community's decision not to tolerate violence——either by strangers or by its own members. As a UN expert group recommended in 1993, acceptance within the community of the responsibility to shame persons publicly who commit such violence can be an effective preventative measure.[2] In order to make this possible, however, it is first necessary to break the silence—to encourage women to speak out and protest the violence in their lives, both personal and public—as many of the chapters in this volume demonstrate. While empowering individual women is an important strategy to reduce women's vulnerability to violence, however, it is not by itself sufficient. Even women who are able to gain enough control over their lives to avoid situations of domestic violence remain vulnerable to violence in the public sphere—either from individual perpetrators or in some cases, from gangs, militias, the police, and even the military.

Communities need models and mechanisms for dealing with violence against women that occur within their own boundaries. Moving towards community responsibility requires strong and enduring community-based organizations, especially but not exclusively women's organizations. Accordingly, national governments and the international development and human-rights community should explore to what extent these groups need assistance in incorporating the eradication of discrimination generally and gender-based violence specifically into their work strategies. Development initiatives should reinforce structures, control mechanisms, or associations—whether formal or informal—that are capable of delegitimizing violence as a means of conflict resolution in the family or in the community.

Creating a sense of public responsibility for gender-based violence also involves examining the ways in which institutions in society currently condone such violence, either actively or by passively looking away.

Schools, religious institutions, workplaces, social clubs, and families, along with the advertising and communications media, must be challenged about their tolerance of, and thus collusion in, the perpetuation of violence against women. The establishment and promotion of uniform international standards of state responsibility and of mechanisms for international monitoring can play an important role in changing institutional structures and practices.

Some may argue—even within the human-rights community—that the state should not intervene in what are considered private or domestic matters. But the state is always involved, explicitly or implicitly, in gender-based violence, both by way of laws and policies that encourage or discourage such violence and by the efforts it exerts or fails to exert to implement those measures. But as one expert notes, "Gender relations are already regulated by states, through fiscal arrangements, social security, immigration law, and marriage and family law, established religion, military service, and executed through all the statutory instruments, administrative procedures, and legal and judicial processes, as well as the executive and elective bodies. It is the duty of 'good governments' to enforce respect for women's human rights within them."[3] State accountability for actively seeking to eradicate violence against women is based on the state's universally recognized responsibility to respect and ensure the fundamental human rights of all individuals in its territory.

Deconstructing Traditional Power Structures and Cultural Assumptions

The subjugation of women, including violence in many forms, is so common in many societies, and so deeply entrenched in many cultural and religious traditions, that it has eluded widespread acceptance as a human-rights issue. And yet, gender-based violence parallels other forms of abuse that are clearly and consistently included in the human-rights discourse. Battery and sexual assault in the home resemble widely recognized forms of torture; rape in public, particularly mass rape, is clearly a form of terrorism; systematic and coercive deprivation of mobility and material resources, combined with strict control of women's labour, parallel conditions that are widely regarded as slavery.

Despite the evident parallels, however, resistance to treating violence against women as a human-rights abuse is common, both by governments and within the larger society. One of the major barriers is the prevalence of cultural and religious norms and values that reinforce and justify existing power structures. Of course, no culture or religion intends to be abusive; the oppressive nature of many of their assumptions lies beneath the surface. Deconstructing the oppressive aspects of such practices, as part of the ongoing process of reinterpreting basic principles, is a crucial step towards eradicating violence against women.

While culture and religion remain barriers to the eradication of violence against women, there are many efforts being made to counter their influence. In countries throughout Latin Americaand the Caribbean, as elsewhere, people are growing more aware of the power of education and the media to challenge and transform social and cultural norms and values, as well as to reinforce and strengthen them. As many of the articles included in this book demonstrate, efforts are growing in many parts of the region to remove gender bias and gender stereotyping from school curricula and teaching materials; to integrate gender-awareness training, parenting skills, and non-violent conflict resolution into school curricula; and to provide gender-awareness training to teachers and educators, including teaching them to recognize signs of abuse. Central to these efforts is the insistence on the principle of the universality of human rights, reaffirmed in the Declaration on the Elimination of Violence Against Women and the Vienna Declaration and Programme of Action at the 1993 World Conference on Human Rights. These rights are declared not to be derogated, meaning that they cannot be limited by reference to custom, tradition or religious consideration.[4]

Throughout Latin America and the Caribbean, women's groups have struggled to broaden the understanding of human rights to include the right to be free of violence, making the issue central to national development agendas. Yet here as elsewhere, they have recognized that despite many improvements—in law, government policy, and education—the problem of gender violence will persist so long as women continue to be devalued in society. This recognition is based in years of work (much of it supported by UNIFEM) with women victims of gender violence, with government ministries, health and education officials, and law enforcement agencies, as well as reflection upon the often frustrating results of this experience. The chapters that follow locate the experience in different countries within the history of efforts to combat gender violence within a broader human-rights framework. Looking at the region as a whole, Marcela Ortiz documents the efforts of national and regional women's movements over two decades to bring the issue of gender violence out of private sphere and into the centre of public discussion. She chronicles a history of legislative reform and public awareness as well as the decision to move from denouncing the problem to researching its causes and documenting its reach. Focussing specifically on criminal laws, Gladys Acosta reviews the ways in which women and women's rights have been conceptualized historically in Latin American criminal law and documents efforts to modernize these concepts in line with the democratization process now underway. Similar efforts, both to document the nature and extent of gender violence and to devise legal and political strategies to combat it, are underway in countries throughout the Caribbean, as Roberta Clarke documents. Taking up sexual offences, domestic violence and sexual harassment separately, she reviews the state of legislation as well as broader efforts by women's groups to change prevailing cultural assumptions about women's roles and present gender violence as a human-rights issue. Looking at the Andean region, Alexandra Ayala Marín reviews progress in implementing international recommendations concerning the prevention of gender violence, focussing on efforts to integrate gender and human-rights training into the institutions of law enforcement and justice administration.

Despite many changes, in law as well as government policy, however, gender violence, far from disappearing, is increasing in almost every country, as subsequent articles show. Patricia Duarte Sánchez and Gerardo González, analysing images and programmes to combat gender violence in Mexico, stress the need to go beyond legal reforms to bring about broader social change. They describe the effort to create an alternative discourse, one which will take the issue of gender violence beyond a struggle between men and women to a wider arena of citizenship and democracy. In Brazil, where domestic violence and sexual abuse are still largely hidden, Heleieth Saffioti reflects on a recent study in São Paulo, where special women's police stations have been set up to deal with such crimes. Because gender violence crosses both race and class lines, she argues, any effort to eliminate it requires systematic intervention by the state. And Cecilia Babb, reviewing the experience of the Rape Crisis Society of Trinidad & Tobago, which has been confronting the issue of sexual violence for over ten years, reflects on the strengths and limitations of such efforts and makes recommendations for their future direction.

The human security of women, and the well-being of their dependents, will rely in large measure on the recognition that societies can alter traditions without sacrificing their identity or stability. It will hinge on the ability of religious and cultural communities to emphasize the core values of love and justice over the patriarchal traditions of the subjugation of women. And it will depend on the incorporation of those values into the legal frameworks of national and international bodies. In 1998, the international community will have another opportunity to renew its commitment to the principles enshrined in the Universal Declaration on Human Rights 50 years ago. Women will have another opportunity to mobilize and demand that governments and the UN put actions behind the promises made in all the international documents and declarations. For there will never be a true culture of respect for human rights without the inclusion of respect for the human rights of women.   ❖

Notes

1. *Report of the World Conference on Human Rights,* Vienna, 14-25 June 1993 (A/CONF. 157/24)

2. *Report of the Expert Group Meeting on Measures to Eradicate Violence Against Women,* New Brunswick, New Jersey, 4-8 October 1993, p. 5, issued by the UN Department of Policy Coordination and Sustainable Development.

3. Georgina Ashworth, "Women and Human Rights," background paper for DAC Expert Group on Women in Development, Organization for Economic Cooperation and Development, Paris, May 1992, p.22.

4. *Report of the Expert Group Meeting on Measures to Eradicate Violence Against Women,* p.7.

Violence Against Women:
A Regional Crisis

MARCELA ORTIZ

*"Ultimately, we are convinced that no single mechanism
will stop violence against women, making the use
of an integrated set of mechanisms essential."*

Throughout the 1980s, as women's groups in Latin America and the Caribbean mobilized around issues concerning the status of women, they increasingly came up against the problem of gender-related violence, which again and again impeded their efforts to move ahead on a range of issues, from health to development. Thus with great dedication and few resources, and facing strong resistance from tradition and culture, they began to document the magnitude of this phenomenon. Many groups formed specifically to work on the issue of violence against women, while at the same time several existing groups began to include this issue in their programmes.

This process triggered the creation of several mechanisms to confront the phenomenon: temporary shelters for women victims of violence, integrated attention centres offering social, legal, psychological and medical assistance, and support and self-help groups. Governments began to open Women's Offices, which due to their national scope, became important public initiatives for promoting actions and programmes to deal with violence against women, especially on the legal front. In several countries they succeeded in setting up women's police stations, a trend that began in 1985 in Brazil and has spread through other countries during the 1990s. And in terms of legislation, women's groups began to push for new laws dealing specifically with violence against women and proposals for reforming criminal codes. At the end of the 1980, Puerto Rico became the first government in the region to approve specific legislation with its 1989 Preventing and Intervening in Domestic Violence Law.

New challenges for the women's movement emerged, too, including the need to advise governments and the obligation to participate actively in international gatherings. With a growing awareness of the need to coordinate and elaborate proposals which integrated both the prevention and eradication of gender violence, women began discussing the possibility of joining forces, talents, experiences, ideas and analyses.

At the same time, women's groups in a number of countries, which had been working on this issue for several years, began to move from denouncing the problem to researching its causes and studying proposals to confront sexual and domestic violence. For regional and international organizations, the issue took on increased importance in the context of human-rights concerns during the 1990s. The 1985 World Conference on Women, held in Nairobi, Kenya, was crucial in this process, and the final document, "Forward Looking Strategies," gave high priority to eliminating violence against women. At a regional level, too, the need to exchange experiences and share access to systematic information combined with a growing awareness of the importance of coordinated efforts at multiple levels to propel the organization of four meetings of Latin American and Caribbean feminists during the 1980s.

At the first of these meetings, which took place in Colombia in July 1981, women selected November 25, the anniversary of the assassination of the Mirabal sisters in the Dominican Republic, as the annual International Day Against All Forms of Violence Against Women. At the second meeting, two years later in Peru, participants in the Workshop on Sexual Slavery and Violence joined the Europe-based International Feminist Network Against Traffic in Women and Female Sexual Slavery, advanced the idea of shelters to help battered women and agreed to coordinate research on violence against women, seen as a social phenomenon common to all the countries of the region. The third meeting in Brazil in 1985 and the fourth in Mexico in 1987 took up the possibility of including the issue of violence against women in the Latin American and Caribbean Women's Health Network's bulletin, incorporating aspects such as racism, domestic violence and human rights.

Meanwhile, research on gender-based violence in the region began to accelerate. In 1988 ISS International, with the support of UNIFEM, began to study different kinds of violence against women in Latin America and the Caribbean. The findings, published in 1990, provided a solid foundation for advocacy and public policy work by presenting facts and figures at the regional level for the first time.

The Southern Cone Network Against Domestic Violence was formed November 25, 1989, during a meeting called by Lugar de Mujer of Argentina and attended by ISIS International, La Casa de la Mujer La Morada of Chile, SOS Mujer of Uruguay as well as women's groups in Buenos Aires, Neuquen and Cordoba in Argentina. And a year later, during the Fifth Meeting of Latin American and Caribbean Feminists in Argentina, the Latin American and Caribbean Feminist Network Against Sexual and Domestic Violence was born. ISIS's project on violence against women, supported by UNIFEM, resulted in the first region-wide research on this subject and facilitated the coordination of the Latin American and Caribbean Network Against Sexual and Domestic Violence.

The Latin American and Caribbean Network Against Sexual and Domestic Violence

In its declaration of principles, the Latin American and Caribbean Network Against Sexual and Domestic Violence defined its membership as "non-government organizations and independent persons who, from a gender-perspective, carry out actions to change situations of sexual and domestic violence experienced by woman in the region, with the goal of linking up with government sectors involved in these problems." Since its creation, the Network has become an effective instrument for achieving the goals established when it was founded. With branches in almost every country in the region, the Network has organized seminars and workshops, coordinated regional campaigns, produced publications and made proposals to governments and at world conferences and fora, among many other activities and initiatives. The 1990s have been particularly fruitful years although the Network has also had to confront considerable obstacles.

Women's organizations from 21 Latin America and the Caribbean countries attended the Network's first meeting in 1992 in Olinda, Brazil. ISIS International was chosen as the Network headquarters, responsible for communications and information with five subregional focal points: Mexico and Central America; Andean (Columbia, Venezuela, Chile, Ecuador, Peru); Brazil and the Southern Cone (Argentina, Paraguay, Uruguay); the Caribbean.

The Network's first priority was to coordinate among the sub-regions and headquarters to exchange work experiences, create new or strengthen existing national networks, and ensure that the presence of this issue was present on the agendas of public and private institutions. Raising public awareness at international, regional and national levels of gender-based violence was another priority. Members agreed to coordinate and co-operate with other international and regional networks, organize meetings at different levels and coordinate international and regional campaigns.

Members decided to publish a quarterly newsletter, *Hojas de Datos* (Fact Sheets), for legislators and journalists and a periodic bibliographic review "Documentas". Another decision was to hold regular meetings to coordinate specific work in conjunction with particular events (such as UN world conferences) and periodically evaluate Network progress. Today, the Network has grown not only in membership, but also in the different type of activities that member groups and institutions organize and develop.

Especially important is the development of national networks and/or coalitions. in many countries of the region that raise public awareness, lobby and negotiate with governments. Examples are the Red contra la Violencia from Nicaragua, Red Chilena contra la Violencia Doméstica y Sexual, Coordinadora Paz para la Mujer from Puerto Rico, Red Argentina contra la Violencia Doméstica y Sexual, Red Uruguaya contra la Violencia, Red Brasilera contra la Violencia Doméstica y Sexual; Red Ecuatoriana contra la Violencia; national coalitions in Venezuela and Mexico.

Network goals are based on the conviction that the extent of violence against women throughout the region requires an integrated response. Central to the Network's strategy has been the use of specific actions, information and lobbying to persuade institutions and public-opinion leaders to consider gender violence a social phenomenon affecting all women, independent of social class; to raise awareness that gender-based violence damages all of society, including men and children, and therefore integrated actions are necessary to deal with it. Ultimately, we are convinced that no single mechanism will stop violence against women, making the use of an integrated set of mechanisms essential. Thus the efforts of women's groups and governmental offices, including the many ministries involved in relevant public policy, must be coordinated. The issue must be present in academic, police and judicial spheres, as wells as the media. Advocacy at international and regional levels, supporting relevant resolutions and working to implement them in national legislation and/or public policies has been another important element of Network strategy. Crucial to these strategies have been the concepts of discrimination against women and girls as the basis for violence against them, racial violence and segregation against the region's indigenous and black women, and the view that this problem involves human-rights issues.

Research, Documentation and Communication

The publication of monthly bulletins and periodic Fact Sheets, along with an updated Directory of Programmes on Violence Against Women in the Latin American and Caribbean region, constitutes an important part of the Network's written history as well as a solid research foundation for education and advocacy work. The Bulletin links organizations and institutions with the Network. ISIS's experience dealing with the issue of violence against women—especially its ongoing systematization of references, statistics and bibliographic material on violence against women in the region and around the world—provided a solid foundation for this effort. A wide variety of groups, ranging from legislators to human-rights organizations, religious institutions and men's organizations against violence against women have shown interest in the Network and its publications, which include:

- A 1990 report, *Violence Against Women in Latin America and the Caribbean: Information and Politics,* defines violence against women and its diverse manifestations (political, work-related, media-related, sexual and domestic violence, the latter being the most common) throughout the region. Written by Teresa Rodríguez, M. Soledad Weinstein, Eliana Largo, Isabel Duque and Gloria Molina, the report revealed how women were responding to violence and proposed policies and programmes to deal with the issue. Data came from analyzing existing documentation and a questionnaire completed by 190 academic, governmental and non-governmental organizations in 22 countries.

- A Bibliographic Catalogue, *Violence Against Women in Latin America and the Caribbean, Bibliographic Catalogue,* published in 1990, contains 350 bibliographic references and their abstracts, with emphasis on publications produced during the 1980, plus 49 international and technical entries.

- A 1990 Programme Directory, *Violence Against Women in Latin America and the Caribbean, Programme Directory,* contains brief descriptions of 109 programmes dealing with violence against women in the region, organized by country, subject and type of institution involved. This publication also listed 261 regional, national and local organizations working on the issue of gender-based violence.

Research carried out by ISIS International with UNIFEM's support provided the springboard for a qualitative leap in regional awareness of this problem. Until then, despite of the existence of important theoretical work, Latin American women had only partial information on the issue. Results of ISIS research were included in a consultation carried out by the Inter-American Women's Commission of the Organization of American States, which culminated in the adoption of the 1994 Inter-American Convention on the Prevention, Punishment, and Eradication of Violence Against Women ("Belem Convention") by the Organization of American States member states.

A specialized Data Base with bibliographic and reference was also created. Until then, the lack of hard data made it impossible to form a comprehensive understanding of the problem of gender violence. A second step in this process occurred early in 1993 when, again with UNIFEM's support, ISIS International set up a professional team to coordinate the Network, selecting, processing and distributing comparable qualitative and quantitative information on this issue, making it available to members of the Network to back up programmes, public information and lobbying with governments. Other goals included promoting the issue of violence against women in development plans and programmes throughout the region, helping to design, execute and evaluate relevant public policy and legal reforms. Network members also put forward the need to treat violence against women as a social problem and an obstacle to development, and advocated women's full participation in national life. They agreed to work towards more interaction between the different entities responsible for confronting this problem.

What Difference Has the Network Made?

The Latin American and Caribbean Network Against Sexual and Domestic Violence has brought together theoretical and practical efforts and has encouraged the coordination of different groups and national networks, respecting their identities and the specific context of their development. One of its main achievements has been to put the issue of violence against women in all its forms on the public agenda in almost every country in the region, obtaining widespread media coverage.

Legislative initiatives, designed to strengthen existing mechanisms or create new ones, include proposing and/or achieving passage of specific laws dealing with the issue, and evaluating existing legislation.[1] Many Network groups or national networks have directly supported the formulation of public policy and contributed to improving public awareness, as well as training judicial and police employees. Groups affiliated to the Network are beginning to raise related issues, including violence against women as a violation of their human rights, child prostitution, trafficking in women, sexual harassment and the effects on women of armed conflicts.

The Sixteen Days of Activism Against Violence Against Women campaign, commemorated each year from November 25 (International Day Against All Forms of Violence Against Women) to December 10 (anniversary of the Universal Declaration of Human Rights), gave rise to activities in almost every country, with national networks and their members playing a major role. These activities include symbolic trials of specific instances of violence, presentation of legislative proposals, seminars and workshops, signature campaigns and news conferences.

Although an important part of the Network's efforts focussed on regional preparation for the Fourth World Conference on Women in Beijing in 1995, it has also worked on other international events. Member groups participated in the 1994 International Conference on Population and Development in Cairo and the 1995 World Social Development Summit in Copenhagen, preparing documents and lobbying government delegates. Recognizing the 1993 World Conference on Human Rights in Vienna as an opportunity to emphasize women's human rights as part of universal human rights, Network members participated in numerous preparatory activities, among them the First Working Meeting of Regional Human Rights Organizations with Women's Programmes (Costa Rica, 1992), sponsored by the Inter-American Human Rights Institute; the Preparatory Conference "La Nuestra" (Costa Rica, 1992), which conducted a regional evaluation of women's human rights, and the UN Latin American and Caribbean Regional Conference (Costa Rica, January 1993). The appointment of a Special Rapporteur on Violence Against Women by the UN General Assembly following the Vienna Conference stimulated the Network's efforts at every level.

Exchanges and Evaluations

At the end of 1993, at the Sixth Latin American and Caribbean Feminist Meeting in El Salvador, the Network evaluated its activities, exchanged information with national networks, distributed information on campaigns and research and began to prepare for the Fourth World Conference on Women in Beijing. A few months later, in March 1994, the Network met in New York, following the meeting of NGOs. For three intense days, members debated a document prepared by ISIS International analyzing violence against women in the region. ISIS prepared an action plan to strengthen the Network's participation in the pre-Beijing process, along with sub-regional and national efforts to fight violence against women. We also discussed coordinating a panel discussion in Beijing to permit the exchange of experiences among regions.

Working with the Comité Latinoamericano de Derechos de la Mujer (Latin American Committee for the Defense of Women's Rights) (CLADEM) and the Women's Programme of the Instituto Latinamericano de Servicios Legales Alternativo (ILSA), the Network organized a Panel on Violence Against Women at the Regional Forum of NGOs held in Mar del Plata, Argentina, in September 1994. A diverse groups of panelists, including black and indigenous women, academics, feminist and lawyers representatives of human-rights and other social organizations and members of national and regional NGO networks, debated strategies and proposals for the Regional Action Plan.

A Network meeting held during the international seminar on Family Violence and Human Rights in Santiago, Chile (December 1994), charted two priorities: the Fourth World Conference on Women, and national and regional work. We added Network proposals to the regional NGO document for presentation to the Regional NGO Forum at Mar del Plata, and the NGO Forum at the Beijing meeting. We also agreed to lobby for the Inter-American Convention of Belem do Pará as a model for other regions, and to work for the signing and ratification of the Convention in every OAS member state.[2] By June 1995, 25 countries had signed the Convention and 22 had ratified it.

In Beijing, the Network participated in the Global Tribunal on Accountability for Women's Human Rights, helping to select and research cases in Latin America and the Caribbean and supporting the Global Panel on Violence Against Women. Preparations for Beijing inspired the Latin American and Caribbean Network Against Sexual and Domestic Violence and catalyzed sub-regional, national and local seminars on the subject. Documents prepared by national networks and Network members brought access to information on events in each country.

Independently of our Beijing-related activities, the network also held other meetings. These include the National Meeting About Family and Sexual Violence, organized by the Mexican Collective to Fight Violence Against Women (COVAC), in Mexico in November 1994, which led to the creation of a National Coordination to fight gender-based violence; a meeting on Police Institutions and Women's Human Rights in Quito, Ecuador, in December 1994, organized by the Centre for Studies and Research on the Mistreatment of Women (CEIMME), with the support of UNIFEM, UNICEF, the Pan American Health Organization (PAHO), and ISIS International, that brought together representatives from police forces around the region.

Other meetings included the First National Meeting of NGOs Supporting Women and Family Police Stations (Ecuador, 1995); the National Meeting of Nicaragua's Network (1995); the National Meeting of the Chilean Network (Santiago, 1996); the First Provincial Meeting of NGOs on the Prevention of Sexual and Domestic Violence, organized by the Argentine Network (1995); the Second National Meeting of the Brazilian Network (Paraiba, 1995); the Southern Cone Sub-Regional Network Meeting (Asunción, 1995); The Andean Sub-Regional Meeting, and national and regional campaigns against gender violence organized by the Brazilian Network, the Peruvian Network, Puerto Rico, Mexico and others.

On their return from Beijing, Network members focussed on national legislation. For example, the Nicaraguan Network presented a draft law with reforms to the Criminal Code to Prevent and Punish Family Violence and in Mexico, COVAC presented draft reforms to the Civil Procedures and Criminal Code on family violence.

At the international level, ISIS International and representatives of the Network have participated in important meetings, among them the International Conference on Family Violence in Amsterdam (October 1994); the First Seminar for Latin America and the Caribbean on Violence Against Women, sponsored by the Inter-American Women's Commission of the Organization of American States, held in Santiago, Chile (December 1994); the Health, Violence and Society Conference, sponsored by the Pan-American Health Organization in Washington (November 1994); and

Violence Against Women: an Obstacle to Development, held in Madrid in June 1995. And in 1995 and 1996 the Network's Coordinator co-organized the ISIS-WICCE Exchange Programme on Violence Against Women in Armed Conflict Situations. Network participation in these events has helped ensure an international balance and allowed us to participate in the definition of objectives and contents, as well as in the selection of participants, especially those from Latin America.

Obstacles and Reflections

While obstacles to achieving Network goals vary according to country, there are certain similarities among all countries. Most serious is the implementation of a structural adjustment model throughout the region that among other things cuts back on social spending, which means that most countries have reduced budgets for fighting violence against women. At the same time, international funding for women's groups working on this issue has also dropped.

We have also had to recognize the enormous weight of a regional culture accustomed to discrimination and violence against women, which in many cases prevents women from filing charges and carrying them through the legal process. Institutional mistreatment from police officers and judges has no doubt exacerbated this problem. Although laws passed by several countries have been an important step forward, we still face significant difficulties when it comes to enforcement. Lack of coordination between police and courts, a lack of training in how to receive victims of violence and lack of financial, technical and human resources for preventive and educational programmes are clear examples of implementation problems.

There are also countries within our region whose governments have not encouraged legislative debate of this problem. In Colombia, draft laws on domestic violence have been tabled as have sexual harassment laws. In Venezuela, Bolivia, Guatemala, the Dominican Republic, and Costa Rica, domestic violence is not considered a crime. Approval of reforms to Penal Codes has come slowly in the few countries which have adopted them. Most countries maintain weak public policies in this area or inadequate policies that do not prevent sexual and domestic violence against women and girls.

Although the issue is not a new one for the media and it does receive TV and radio coverage, the magnitude of the problem requires much greater information. Governmental campaigns on the issue have been insufficient and require greater presence, outreach and permanence. We have advanced in efforts to bring together NGOs and governments, but the need to improve coordination between these entities to ensure maximum effectiveness and the best use of resources remains urgent. A central demand for women's groups is that official institutions include specific programmes on violence against women and girls designed and implemented in conjunction with NGOs and women's groups, and that governments assume responsibility for training government staff who work with the victims of mistreatment.

The region's ethnic diversity creates additional dimensions to the continuing problem of violence against women, specifically the situation of black and indigenous women. These are doubly marginalized, as they face continuing racism along with violence and are also limited to only the lowest paying jobs. Trafficking in women is most frequent among black women in the region. Policies and programmes which don't take these conditions into consideration simply exclude huge sectors of the population from attempted solutions.

Finally, the political violence which the region has experienced during the past decade in countries such as Chile, Argentina, Uruguay, Brazil, Colombia, El Salvador, Peru, Guatemala and recently Haiti and Mexico (in the southern state of Chiapas), has had high social and human costs for women. Cases of aggression and rape suffered by Haitian and Chiapan women demand further efforts and specific measures from governments and the international community.

Looking Towards the Future

Politically, six years' experience has reaffirmed the need for a Network to coordinate strategies to prevent violence against women. Multiple responses and mechanisms must be developed and this work must be extended and/or consolidated in other fields, such as formal education, the media and human-rights organizations. Persistent violence against women and girls in Latin America and the Caribbean increasingly forces us to emphasize the underlying causes: relationships of hierarchy and power; cultures which undervalue all that is female; unequal opportunities for women. We must build an institutional and social culture that opposes violence against women and girls. Governments and organizations capable of influencing the cultural changes that women and our societies require for full social and human development have a particular responsibility in this process. For this reason, we must focus specific kinds of work on these entities.

There is no doubt that we have made great advances in the past decade. Today we have a well-organized Network prepared to propose, negotiate and act. Nevertheless, given the enormous magnitude of this problem in every country in our region, this work is and will be just beginning — for a very long time.   ❖

Notes

1. Laws specifically dealing with violence against women have been passed in the Bahamas, 1991; Barbados, 1992; Peru, 1993; Argentina, 1994; Chile, 1994; and Ecuador, 1995. Draft laws are under consideration in Colombia, Nicaragua, Mexico and Costa Rica, among others. In 1990, Mexico approved amendments to the Penal Code, which penalize sexual harassment; Brazil and Costa Rica approved a law against sexual harassment; and Trinidad and Tobago approved a law covering sexual offenses.

2. The Inter-American Convention to Prevent, Eradicate and Eliminate Violence Against Women, approved by the OAS in June 1994, was first considered during the First Inter-American Consultation on Women and Violence in 1990, organized by the Interamerican Women's Commission of the OAS, with the participation of several Network members.

Women's Human Rights and Latin American Criminal Law

GLADYS ACOSTA VARGAS

"The World Conference on Human Rights in Vienna in 1993 enshrined women's rights within the heart of the human-rights doctrine; culture and history can no longer justify limitations on women's rights."

Despite the democratization process of the last two decades, the human-ness of women is still in the process of construction throughout Latin America. Nowhere is this more evident than in the criminal-law codes, which remain anchored in the past, confining women to "social prisons" constructed by cultural and religious prejudice. A review of the criminal codes of 19 Latin American countries, undertaken by UNIFEM and UNICEF, highlights the enormous distance between these antiquated codes and the increasingly advanced international documents, whether binding conventions or statements of principles. [1]

For women to become full citizens in Latin America, the legal codes must abandon the practice of defining women in terms of their sexuality, or as creatures who require a guardian to take care of them. The patriarchal goal of controlling "women's disorder" by banishing them to the realm of nature (Pateman 1989), can no longer be viewed as a legitimate function of the state.

Over the last decade, the United Nations has opened up a major political opportunity for expanding women's human rights. The Universal Declaration of 1948, a fundamental first step towards guaranteeing minimum human rights, needed to be construed "through a woman's eyes" in order to achieve the universal aims that inspired it. Since the Decade for Women (1975-1985), a series of UN Conferences have shown that

---

This article has been translated from the more extensive document, La mujer en los codigos penales de America Latina y el Caribe Hispano *(1996), a joint publication of UNIFEM and UNICEF, which lists the relevant laws in each country and where they can be obtained.*

discrimination against women is a worldwide phenomenon, expressed at all levels of social life. The 1993 World Conference on Human Rights in Vienna enshrined women's rights within the heart of the human-rights doctrine, making clear that culture and history can no longer justify limitations on women's rights.

As a result of these historic conferences, all countries have an obligation to revise their legal systems in accordance with international mandates. Legislatures must take the responsibility of amending criminal codes, drawing on the contributions of women's movements in this process. Women's movements need encouragement in the struggle to formulate legal amendments and negotiate their passage through domestic legislative bodies. It is time to ask whether the notions of women's status enshrined in criminal codes accord with the broad, participatory democratic principles of Latin American societies.

Integrating Gender into the Democratization Process

A critical reading of criminal codes cannot ignore the historical context in which they were written. Laws in every society reflect the interest of those in power. In democratic societies, however, the evolution of these laws also reflects an ongoing struggle between different social forces. With regard to laws concerning the status of women, those forces opposed to change have been until recently overwhelmingly powerful. Thus criminal codes are loaded with archaic standards regarding women. It is unbelievable that at the end of the 20th century, abortion with informed consent is forbidden, while infanticide by the mother or close relatives is not, if the desire to protect family "honour" is involved. Virginity is still sanctified. And abusive violence is not recognized as a crime so long as it occurs within the family.

During the last half of the 20th century it has become possible to "internationalize" the grounds for human-rights standards, which are now based on broad international consensus. International human-rights conventions, once signed and ratified by nation-states, entail a commitment to build international standards into domestic legislative life. Nevertheless, the amendment process is slow and uneven, requiring the expansion of broad social awareness and an opening of the legislative process in each country. What is needed is a broad gender perspective, stepping back from advocacy of patriarchal interests and recognizing women's and men's rights, in all their diversity, to formulate different ways of analyzing reality and proposing legislative solutions (CEMUJER 1995). The goal, as Peruvian attorney Giulia Tamayo has argued, is to find new ways to build justice into people's daily lives, integrating justice into all institutions of society. Indeed, a change in institutional norms means admitting that there is no single way to resolve the contradictions and tensions generated by women's demands; rather these depend on conditions in each society (Jelin 1993:60).

International Discourse on Specific, Concrete Rights

The last few years have witnessed the broad recognition within the international community of gender analysis as a key category through which to examine the enjoyment of human rights, particularly in drafting instruments designed to eliminate discrimination against women.[2] However, as in other areas of human rights, there is a gap between ideal and reality. The most general standards, such as the Universal Declaration of Human Rights and the international agreements, have been reinterpreted within regional frameworks. In Latin America, the American Declaration on the Rights and Duties of Man in 1948 and the American Convention on Human Rights (San José Pact) in 1969 comprise the basis for human-rights protection in the region. And the Inter-American Convention to Prevent, Sanction and Eradicate Violence Against Women in 1994 is an example of the application of gender analysis to the formulation of regional legislation to protect and respond to the needs of the female population.

Recognizing their potential for broadening the notion of fundamental rights, Latin American women's groups have worked to breath life into international mandates, proposing ways to adapt national norms to their standards.[3] While unlike treaties, world conference documents are not binding, they are expressions of international consensus and, as such, may inspire state policy, providing the government has not objected to the wording at the time of its approval. This process of "appropriation" of international laws must be complemented by a political strategy to mobilize civil and governmental sectors to achieve the legislative transformations that will make the law an efficient instrument to improve women's position.

Women in Latin America's Criminal-Law Codes

The treatment of women in criminal-law codes reflects the way in which their role is conceptualized in Latin American societies. According to the almost uniform wording of criminal law norms in the region, women embody a series of physiological, social and psychological conditions that make them "victims" to be protected. Women are subordinate for reasons "based on nature," and viewed as beings who must be taken care of, given their psycho-physical "instability" (Laqueur 1990; Lagarde 1996). If we accept that criminal-law codes formalize socially unacceptable behaviour, we must identify criteria by which norms may be transformed. Lack of enforcement is not sufficient to bring about change, since the norm-setting system is a major symbolic referent and requires autonomy from justice administration per se.

Throughout the criminal codes, the concept of women as subordinate emerges through biological, social and economic definitions of women's experience. Notions about women's biology not only underlie the criminalization of abortion, but also inform the provision of extenuating circumstances in cases of crimes against life as a result of hormonal influences specific to women. Social notions of manhood and womanhood underpin crimes against honour as well as the lack of protection for sexual freedom and the failure to address domestic violence. Concepts of male and female economic roles underlie the provision of such crimes as failure to provide food as well as the lack of provision for abortion in the case of need.

Abortion and Infanticide

With the exception of Cuba, the criminal codes of all countries in Latin America views abortion as a crime against life and personal security. This does not apply to spontaneous miscarriage, which occurs without human intervention and may be caused by physical, emotional or pathological disturbances.

The criminal codes regarding abortion also recognize extenuating circumstances, as when women have abortions in order to conceal their dishonour (Art. 81, para 2, Argentina; Art. 120 Costa Rica) or when they become pregnant due to violent or abusive carnal knowledge or through artificial insemination without their consent (Art. 345 Colombia). Other extenuating circumstances include pregnancies that result from rape out of wedlock or artificial insemination without consent that has occurred out of wedlock (Art. 120 Peru). Abortion caused by economic desperation, though it is one of the most common motives among the underprivileged sectors, is recognized as an extenuating circumstance only in Uruguay, which it is included among the reasons already noted (Art. 328, para 4).

Restrictions on the capacity to decide about reproduction extend even to the right to information about birth-control methods. This is true in

Costa Rica, which considers it a crime to advertise procedures or substances intended to prevent pregnancy (Art. 374, para 6). The Dominican Republic makes criminally liable one who puts the pregnant woman in contact with another person who will cause the abortion, providing the abortion actually occurs (Art. 317).

The Cuban criminal code, however, allows abortion under health regulations. An abortion is only punishable when performed outside these regulations. The penalty is more serious if it is performed for money or outside official institutions or by someone who is not a physician (Art. 7). The code also penalizes anyone who purposely provokes abortion, with or without violence towards the pregnant woman (Art. 8). In so doing it exercises oversight of women's freedom of choice while also safeguarding her own life.

Physiological changes due to biology, whether transitory or permanent, are given greater attention in the case of women, who are categorized according to their hormonal development: as a maiden, a pregnant woman, a woman in labour, a newly delivered mother, or a woman in menopause. Character changes are commonly defined as menstrual depressions, hysterical states, menopause-related, with a connotation of vulnerability due to nature. Normal biological situations seem to take on another dimension and call for treatment of mental disturbances comparable to psychic handicaps or transitory pathological states.[4]

Criminal laws include extenuating circumstances for women on the basis of their supposed physiological vulnerability (Art. 52 Cuba). Among crimes against life and well-being there is recurrent mention of post-partum depression that qualifies for reduction of penalties in the case of infanticide by the mother (Art. 155 El Salvador). In Mexico, post-delivery "emotional states" are an extenuating factor in the case of infanticide only if the infant has not been registered with the Civil Registry, that is, before its legal existence has begun (Art. 327). The Guatemalan Code regards a woman's pathological "reduction to nature" as an extenuating factor in the case of a mother who, driven by motives linked intimately to her pregnant condition and unquestionably upset, abandons her child within three days of birth (Art. 155)

The integration within criminal codes of extenuating factors and exemptions from penalty reveals an express notion of social responsibility, implemented by men, for women's sexuality, especially within the institution of marriage or parenthood, which gives women a male guardian.

The greatest legally protected value, i.e. human life, takes second place when the perpetrator acts to protect the women's "honour" or that of her closest relatives.

Provisions regarding infanticide make it evident that the norm used to criminalize abortion, protection of the fetus' life, is meaningless, since protecting that life once it is born depends on whether or not its conception affected the family's "honour." "Family honour may be defended" not only by the mother but also by her husband, or her son, father or brother. Such considerations override the weight granted to life, even if the mother of the newborn wishes otherwise (Art. 413 Venezuela; Art. 453 Ecuador). Such circumstances apply only in the period immediately following birth, since they depend on the birth being concealed from public knowledge as well as the alleged "abnormality" of the woman's physiological state: in general, the homicide must take place "during the delivery or while under the influence of the birth process" (Arts. 258, 252 Bolivia; Art. 4 Cuba; Art. 123 Honduras).

If the newborn is abandoned rather than killed, there are extenuating factors when the reason relates to honour (Art. 279 Bolivia; Art. 107 Argentina; Art. 439 Venezuela). In Colombia, there is a reduction of penalty for abandonment when the child is the outcome of rape or artificial insemination without consent (Art. 347), although this becomes more serious if the abandonment is followed by injury or death (Art. 348).[5]

One exceptional situation extends the provisions regarding abandonment to include those responsible for impregnating a woman who abandon her while she is in a critical situation. This appears to be an attempt to protect the woman (Art. 150 Peru).

In some countries, such as Ecuador, the criminal code provides for a sort of "authorization" to commit crimes against life when it is a matter of honour. In most cases, this applies to men who defend the honour of "their" women, since the reverse situation is not provided for. There is considered to be no infraction in cases of injuries to a spouse or the other party when surprised in flagrant adultery (Art. 22 Ecuador). In Uruguay, this is included under reasons for impunity, empowering the judge to nullify the penalty when a perpetrator kills or injures a spouse caught in flagrante, or kills the accomplice because of "passion provoked by the adultery," providing that he has "a good record" (Art. 36). Similar norms are inscribed in the laws of the Dominican Republic (Art. 324) and Nicaragua (Art. 130). Penalties are reduced for the husband, father or grandfather (Art. 423 Venezuela) or for elder brothers and fathers of daughters under age 21 (Art. 129 Nicaragua). In Mexico, the penalty is reduced to a minimum of three days (Arts. 310 and 311).

Lack of Protection for Sexual Freedom

The patriarchal bias involved in the "proper manners," "honourability" and "chastity" required of women lead to certain "virtues" depending on whether or not they are married, and treat women as objects, rather than bearers of legal rights, such as personal well-being or freedom. There is a scale in rating women in terms of chastity, honourability and good manners: first young girls, then adolescent girls, then married women, followed by chaste women with good reputations (i.e. unmarried and virgin), followed by deflowered women and finally by prostitutes, whatever their age (Art. 315 Paraguay). Many of these criteria do not appear in the laws, but pervade the judicial mentality used to interpret them. The crime of slander is considered to involve the disclosure of doubts regarding the woman's chastity (Art. 173 Nicaragua), suggesting that "chastity" is the supreme good with regard to a woman's "honour."

Rape, seduction and abduction

In all criminal codes, the crime of rape—violent sexual acts—involves the use of violence to consummate the sexual relationship. The variants are applied as a function of the victim's characteristics, regarding age or mental health. While victims may be male or female, when the woman is considered to be the victim, the rape is defined as having sexual relations using violence, which she cannot prevent, or if she is under age 12 (Art. 173 Guatemala) or 14 (Art. 213 Brazil). The laws of Cuba punish the person who has sexual relations with a woman, either normally or against nature, using force or sufficient intimidation; or if the victim is mentally handicapped or has some mental disturbance or no reason or sense, or cannot present resistance or lacks the capacity to understand the repercussions of her action or to guide her behaviour (Art. 298). Dominican legislation punishes someone who has "normal and illicit carnal knowledge" of a person of the female sex against the latter's wishes (Art. 332). The requirement of both normalcy and illicitness makes sense only if it is interpreted to mean that the rape is committed outside marriage. Salvadoran legislation prescribes that only women can be victims of rape (Art. 192). Carnal access to females under age 12 is also considered rape (even with consent) or when the victim is physically or mentally unable to offer resistance (Art. 193 El Salvador). This law considers rape to be "carnal access by the male in another male or in a woman by the improper route" if the circumstances of the rape coincide.

Some criminal-law codes consider that the victim may be male or female (Art. 140 Honduras; Art. 308 Bolivia; Arts. 298, 300 Colombia). Colombia is the only country that punishes, as a crime against personal autonomy, artificial insemination of a woman without her consent (Art. 280).

The laws of Peru consider rape as the carnal act practiced with violence or a serious threat and establish four to eight years' imprisonment (Art. 120). There could be rape within marriage. However, when dealing with abortion, the penalty is extenuated when the pregnancy is the consequence of rape out of wedlock or artificial insemination without consent that has occurred out of wedlock. This shows that, if such acts occur within a valid marriage, the woman would not be entitled to the extenuation of the penalty in the event of abortion. This, then, constitutes discrimination according to marital status.

Among extenuating factors for the crime of rape is if the victim is a prostitute, in which case the penalty can be reduced by up to one fifth (Art. 393 Venezuela; Art. 196 El Salvador).

All criminal laws consulted provide for the crime of "estupro" (ravishment), sexual relations with a consenting male or female minor, in general providing that the person be "chaste." Although the victim may be of either sex, the penalties are directly related to the notion of "virginity," which women are culturally the bearers of, as a supreme value. In the laws of Brazil, for example, "estupro" is described as having carnal access to a "chaste woman" through fraud; no age is determined, although age is a contributing factor to the seriousness of the crime. Thus, if the woman is a virgin aged 14 to 18 years, the penalty doubles (Art. 215 Brazil). There is also a penalty for someone who induces a chaste woman, through fraud, to practice or allow a libidinous act to be practiced with her. If the victim is between 14 and 18 years of age, the penalty is worse (Art. 216).

When the law stipulates that it is a crime to seduce a "virgin woman," from 14 to 18 years of age, obtaining carnal access, taking advantage of her inexperience or justifiable trust, it is clear that the law is acting as guardian for the virginity of women under age 18, as opposed to their will or the exercise of their sexuality (Art. 217 Brazil; Art. 309 Bolivia).

Another variety is presented in the laws of Uruguay, which consider "estupro" to be carnal knowledge with a "maiden girl" from 15 to 20 years of age, on the basis of a promise of marriage, and also if the woman is over 20, providing she is a maiden and that marriage is "feigned for this purpose" (Art. 275). That is, premarital virginity is treated as the object of special guardianship, beyond the woman's age or wishes, and the framework of marriage for the exercise of her sexuality. In Honduras, "estupro" involves sexual relations with a "maiden" between 12 and 21 years, with unfair use of authority or trust. There is also a penalty for any other unchaste abuse committed under these circumstances (Art. 142).

"Abduction" is one of the crimes that most clearly shows that the guardianship of women, as people, is not the point. The woman's wishes or decisions are not taken into account. What is protected is the role that women play within the family. And they can exercise their freedom and sexuality only if they marry. Moreover, if there is a "happy ending" no crime has occurred

The crimes of rape, ravishment and abduction go unpunished in most criminal law codes if the infractor marries the victim, once the latter is returned to a safe place (the family) and her consent is obtained. In the case of Colombia, if the rape has been committed by several people, and any one of them marries the victim, this brings an end to the criminal-law action for all of the rapists (Art. 307). This shows that women and their psycho-physical well-being and sexual freedom are not being protected; the safeguards are for the role allocated to women as wives. No other explanation accounts for this pardon through marriage, which exists in the laws of Honduras (Art. 151); Guatemala (Art. 200); Argentina (Art. 132); Colombia (Art. 307) Panama (Art. 225), Venezuela (Art. 395); and Ecuador (Art. 532).[6]

Sexual harassment

Only Cuba provides for sexual harassment as a crime (Art. 301). In many countries, the issue is addressed in other parts of the law, such as labour-related or civil-law affairs, when for example sexual harassment results in the loss of a job or an indemnity. This approach seems appropriate; because of the preventive effect of knowing, for example, that sexual harassment can result in the loss of a job or position, this may be more persuasive. However, this would exclude those who are self-employed bosses, such as in the common case of domestic maids, who are subjected to sexual harassment by the household males. Cuba recognizes sexual harassment in the behaviour of any authority, functionary or employee who proposes sexual relations to a woman who is under their authority having been arrested, imprisoned, penalized or taken into custody; to the wife, daughter, mother, sister or similar relative of a person under such a situation; and also regarding women who have a civil lawsuit, cause or process, etc. of any nature that is pending resolution, processing, or the issue of an official opinion or report, in which the harasser must be involved because of his position (Art. 302 Cuba).

The laws of Mexico address this issue most precisely, under the heading of crimes against freedom and normal psycho-sexual development. This punishes persons who, for lascivious purposes, repeatedly pressure a person of either sex, using their hierarchical position deriving from their labour, educational, domestic or any other such relation entailing subordination. It adds that if the harasser is a public servant and uses the means or circumstances provided by his position he shall be removed from that position. This behaviour is punishable when damages are caused and the claim can be filed only by the party offended (Art. 259a).

Prostitution or acts of corruption

Most criminal-law codes punish those who induce to acts of prostitution (Art. 388 Venezuela). Punishment is specified for those who induce minors, even if the minors consent (Art. 188 Guatemala; Art. 125 Argentina) or those who by apparently legitimate promises lead to the prostitution or corruption of a minor (Art. 190 Guatemala; Art. 309 Colombia; Art. 167 Costa Rica; Art. 201 Nicaragua; Art. 228 Panama; Art. 179 Peru). However, the notion of chastity restricts the rights of women who practice prostitution and, although not always explicitly formulated, criminal law doctrine identifies chaste women as not being prostitutes.

Criminalization of Extramarital Relations

In almost all bodies of law, adultery is considered a crime, although it may sound hypocritical, in view of the social reality. However, this would be nothing more than just another norm out of joint with reality, if there were not the additional gender difference in these laws, as to what constitutes adultery (Art. 396 Venezuela; Art. 216 Nicaragua). In general, women consummate the crime of adultery by simply having an extramarital sexual relationship, whereas men are adulterers only if they engage in a stable relationship (concubinage) with another woman; in some laws, even that is not enough, and the concubinage must occur within the marital household to be considered adultery (Art. 118 Argentina; Art. 5 El Salvador). Adultery is a paradigmatic situation regarding differences between men and women in sexual terms and in the expectations for male and female roles.

Domestic Violence

When domestic violence causes damage to the body or health, this behaviour comes under the crime of causing injury, provided for under all these laws, and classified according to the seriousness of the damage as slight, serious or very serious. The penalty for this crime, in almost every country's law, is more serious when there is a family relationship between the infractor and victim. Abuse in the home is treated as a separate problem and as a crime in the Venezuelan laws (Art. 420; Art. 408) and as a misdemeanor in the laws of Peru (Art. 442); Honduras (Arts. 398; 399); Guatemala (Art. 483) and Chile (Art. 397).

Criminal lawsuits cannot be brought when there are procedural norms prohibiting such actions between spouses, as is the case in Ecuador. Bolivia prescribes no penalties in cases of slight injuries caused by spouses, offspring, parents, siblings and so on, by direct family line, and in-laws living under the same roof. This provides impunity for violence within families, providing the outcome is not very serious. Other manifestations of domestic violence are ignored, as in the case of aggression against the property of the person affected. In Honduras, theft, fraud or damage caused by one spouse against the other, by those living together as such, and by blood relatives or in-laws are absolved of criminal-law liability (Art. 264).

In general, protection for women would be greater if the penalties were more serious when there is a family relationship between infractor and victim, than when the crime does not involve the family circle.

Economic Conditions

Criminal law provides certain norms regarding personal and family property, penalizing failure to perform family obligations, either for both spouses or only for the man. As for failure to provide food, one of the typical crimes in which the woman is the victim and requires protection, criminal law provisions are generally quite broad and easily dodged by offenders. Peru considers it a crime that anyone can commit against a family, and describes it as the failure to fulfill the obligation to provide the food or alimony set forth in a court ruling. The crime is worse if the infractor has simulated another food-related obligation in connivance with a third party or if he maliciously resigns from or abandons his job (Art. 149). Moreover, the need for a court ruling greatly limits the possibility of punishing this crime, because women are often unable to obtain such rulings. In other cases, the crime is subject to proof of an "authentication" requirement," allowing tremendous leeway for interpretation (Art. 177 Honduras).

Bolivia features another concept which does not appear elsewhere: it considers the infractor to be anyone who makes a woman pregnant out of wedlock and abandons her without providing the necessary assistance. The penalty is worse if, as a consequence, the woman commits the crime of abortion, infanticide or abandonment of the newborn, or commits suicide. This is one of the few norms that envision male responsibility (Art. 250).

The laws of Guatemala are the most restrictive, calling for a definite judgement or agreement in a public or authentic document to punish one who refuses to meet his obligations after having been legally summoned to do so, unless he can prove that he is economically unable to do so (Art. 242). Lack of income can be grounds for a judge to remove the obligation to pay in Panama (Art. 213).

Guidelines for Criminal Law Reform with a Gender Perspective

There can be little doubt that all Latin American criminal-law codes are a projection of discrimination and foster the continued subordination of women, reflecting society's inequalities. Laws come to life when applied to real-life conflicts, for both victims and offenders. General terms become particular when applied to women's experience with criminal law institutions and procedures.[7] However, it also harmful to maintain those norms that are no longer enforced in existing criminal-law.[8] A democratic system must develop appropriate consultation mechanisms to keep norms constantly up to date.

In order to put international human-rights standards into practice, the following discriminatory "pearls," selected from numerous studies by women's movement scholars and activists, must be eliminated from criminal-law codes.

Decriminalization of Behaviour Grounded in Reproductive Freedom

Abortion and access to means of sterilization require realistic treatment at arms-length from moralistic and religious positions. The Fourth World Conference on Women has proposed to governments that it will be necessary to amend legislation that punishes women who undergo an abortion voluntarily, and to guarantee that they can exercise their reproductive rights by eliminating coercive laws. Women's Human Rights include the right to control and decide freely about matters involving sexuality (including sexual and reproductive health) in the absence of coercion, discrimination and violence.

Decriminalization of interruption of undesired pregnancy. Decriminalization based on time limits (generally three months) is the most suitable position. Another mode used in some Latin American countries is the system of indications (or reasons) that may provide exceptional grounds for authorizations to interrupt a pregnancy with safeguards for the woman's health.

If conditions do not allow overall regulatory de-penalization and application of the time-period system, the possibility of incorporating the indications system could be considered; that is, to authorize interruption of pregnancy in the most urgent cases: fetal malformation (eugenesic abortion), pregnancy resulting from rape (legal or ethical abortion), danger to the life or permanent damage to the health of the mother (therapeutic abortion) and dire economic reasons (social abortion).[9]

The penalties that must be maintained are for those who practice intentional abortion without women's consent, or endanger their lives by failing to have the qualifications or means to perform the operation without risks (Arts. 267 and 268 of Cuba) as well as those who impose the practice of sterilization without the consent of the person involved. There should also be punishment for unpremeditated abortion, which occurs after pregnant women have been treated violently, by an aggressor who is aware of the pregnancy.

Certainly theoretical discussion about the importance of life is relevant. An embryo can be seen as a potentially live human being. The important thing is to point out that in the undeniable conflict of interests between respect for women's rights to decide when they want to become mothers and protection for the embryo's right to live while dependent on the woman's body, the state must take a position. The position defending quality of life, and not just life as a biological entity, would advocate the possibility of interrupting pregnancy, so that women from all levels of society can gain access to adequate services, without risking their lives, as is currently the case, especially for those whose income levels are too low to pay for health services that could offer some freedom from risk. Thus according to international mandates, women's lives cannot continue to be jeopardized for reasons of pregnancy (Plata 1995).

It would seem to be relatively easier to obtain authorization to perform voluntary sterilizations for men and women. Current population policies reveal greater permissiveness for this mode of fertility regulation in several countries that are quite reluctant to change their legal treatment of abortion. In this case, sterilization as such, although it does interrupt a natural function, is not judged to be the mutilation of a vital organ. In any event, voluntary sterilization merits consideration as an option, providing there are conditions for people to make a clear decision. Therefore, voluntary sterilization should be de-penalized.

Repeal of "Extenuating Circumstances" Based on Women's Biology

Infanticide under extenuating circumstances ("honouris causa" and because of recent delivery) is the prototype of distortion in criminal-law doctrine and practice. Characterization of the period immediately following childbirth as a state of psychic disturbance that can cloud women's thinking, and extending this condition to relatives who commit the crime in order to protect the family's "honour," is a denial of protection for life.

The crime of infanticide should have no extenuating circumstances related to honour. No female physiological state should be considered a pretext to justify taking another life. It is incongruent that infanticide should involve a lighter penalty than abortion, within a system that supposedly values protection of life. Moreover, there is no valid reason to maintain extenuating circumstances based on supposed state of insanity accompanying the post-childbirth period. Hormonal changes after delivery do not result in any such anomaly of themselves (although, like any hormonal change in women's life-cycles, they do affect their affective state and psyche). According to physicians and legal specialists, social factors, such as gender roles, can generate severe disturbances. For example, hormonal changes during menopause can make women emotionally volatile in part because they can no longer perform the role of reproduction. While there may be psychic imbalances during the childbirth period it is not childbirth per se, but probably óne of the causes that would be an extenuating circumstance in any criminal-law situation. There could be transitory mental instability during this period, but not as a direct result of delivery itself.

The legal concept of "honour," a social notion linked to control of women's sexual behaviour by their husbands, fathers and brothers, must be removed from criminal-law codes because it is a way of maintaining male control over women and justifying the serious manifestations of domestic violence.[10] This would also prevent the use of this excuse as a specific extenuating circumstance for homicides by family members against women or the person found with her "in flagrant adultery," and for the crime of infanticide committed by mothers and relatives right after childbirth.

The extenuating allegation of "violence emotion" regarding crimes against life it the only one that could be relevant for such cases, if the situation had so seriously affected a person's psychological state as to reduce all inhibitions. This circumstance could be the result of any train of events that lead the person to such a mental state.

Crimes against honour include "adultery," which must also be repealed. Nor can "honour" be considered an extenuating factor for cases in which family members oblige women to abort against their will.

Placing such a high value on family "honour" undermines legal protection for life; by contrast with abortion, in cases of "honouris causa" infanticide and homicide due to adultery, people are killed for "moral" rather than legal reasons. This also jeopardizes women, because it is grounded in a discriminatory social rule. Although some codes of law do not distinguish between men and women as the infractors, the results will still tend to be discriminatory, since extramarital (and premarital) sexual relations tend to be condemned more strongly in women than men by society.

Abandonment of newborns in some criminal-law codes is also grounded in the underlying concept of protecting honour and makes the protection of life conditional on birth registration, because only unregistered children can be abandoned this way. Comparing penalties for voluntary abortion with those for abandonment of newborns for reasons of protecting family honour, there is a logical inconsistency with legal guarantees of the right to life.

Treatment to Protect Motherhood During Prison Terms

Age, health conditions and circumstances involving motherhood must remain in criminal law as protective measures. The reasons to determine how women serve their prison terms must avoid any mention of their "chastity" and ensure general conditions of a humanitarian nature.

Protection for Sexual Freedom as Part of Personal Prerogative

Modern criminal law cannot be built to protect moral concepts or religious ideas, but rather to safeguard social relations among individuals. Human sexuality is fundamentally relational and must take place under conditions of respect for personal rights and freedoms. Consequently, the legal rights protected must be personal safety and sexual freedom, rather than chastity or good manners. So-called sexual crimes harm personal esteem, leaving severe psycho-physical scars (CEMUJER 1995). Such crimes are an example of the abuse of sexual freedom and an expression of lack of respect for the other person. Criminal law intervenes to resolve the conflict between one person's freedom and possible abuses by others. Thus is it critical to consider intimidation, use of force or the circumstances of the victim (age, family and social status, level of subordination).

References to "honour," "chastity" and "good manners" must be removed, and replaced by explicit, concrete, individualized protection for personal safety and sexual freedom. The question of whether protection should be provided for sexual freedom (Bustos 1986: 132) or for personal security (Chejter 1990: 190-91) depends on the concept of sexuality. Identification of crimes that affect sexuality is not simply a technical matter. Criminal-law reform inspired by human rights must express the integrated concept of criminal-law protection for such crimes. Thus crimes against personal security and sexual freedom must come after crimes against life.

Regarding rape, it is important to discuss whether there is rape within marriage. Clearly, civil-law provisions about "conjugal obligations" cannot be used as an excuse to deprive women of their rights. Therefore, married women must be able to denounce their husbands if raped by them. Moreover, although women are generally specified as the victim of this type of aggression, men can also be raped. Thus the definition should cover both eventualities.

Without undermining the force of the law, it is important to not describe all modes of sexual penetration in voyeuristic terms (Chejter 1990). Instead the definition should cover a full range of coerced sexual abuse. It must be recognized that sexual assault also includes elements of power, control and violence and not only sexual behaviour (Soto Cabrera 1988). There has certainly been progress in the newer bodies of law, such as in Peru, which incorporates (Art. 170) a broader definition of the crime of rape: "To use violence or serious threat to force someone to practice a sexual act or some analogous act," leaving it to the judge to decide which acts should be considered as rape. However, this does not yet provide sufficient protection.

The boundaries between rape and "unchaste abuse" are not so clear-cut as claimed by the doctrine that assigns an absolute value to male penetration. The statements of victims of sexual aggression indicate that it may be equally traumatic to experience ejaculation on the body without vaginal penetration. If the intention is to protect people from sexual aggression, it is necessary to include modes of aggression that are just as damaging as penetration, and to expand the capacity of judges to appreciate this reality. To do so it is fundamental to value victims' viewpoints more highly, rather than understanding acts solely in terms of their social nature.

Any sort of legal reform regarding rape must also re-examine procedures, since victims experience denial of their rights in all countries of the region (Siles Vallejos 1995). A proper handling of regulations regarding rape will be essential if other crimes involving personal and sexual security are to be suitably addressed.

Although many women favor repeal of "estupro," this would eliminate protection for young people (ages 12 through 18) who consent to sexual relations with people above them, on the basis of deceit or blackmail. *What should be eliminated is allusion to chastity,* so that criminal-law protection will agree with international standards outlined in the Children's Rights Convention, which protect people in terms of their age rather than their behaviour.

The extensive practice of sexual abuse by parents, close relatives or people charged with children's custody and care calls for the addition of aggravating factors for crimes affecting the sexuality of minors. It is irrelevant to argue whether to include incest; if sexual relations occur as a result of coercion and the abuse of power, they must be punished, whatever the family relationship. Aggravating factors must be maintained for parents, teachers or persons who take advantage of their authority or position, and disqualification of such offenders to act as children's guardians or otherwise *in loco parentis.*

Abduction, which is also considered a crime against honesty, must be repealed. The crime of kidnapping must protect the legal right of "individual freedom" without moral conditions. There is no justification for penalties to be lighter when people are kidnapped for sex or forced marriage than for other reasons. *What must be eliminated is pardon by the offended party as a cause for annulment of the criminal-law liability, in crimes against sexual freedom.* It is archaic to believe that one way to repair the damage caused by sexual aggression could be for the victim to marry the aggressor.

The crime of "adultery" must be repealed. Romantic feelings are a personal, private matter, and should not be subject to legal regulation. Nor should adultery be a reason for legal separation or divorce in civil proceedings. Legal recognition of such behaviour perpetuates de facto discrimination against women, even where the norm purportedly covers adultery by husbands and wives both. Maintaining a distinction such as in Argentine law (Navarro 1992:379) makes the formal discrimination evident, but does not significantly alter the results.

Redefinition of the Crime of Family Abuse

Legal recognition of domestic violence against women implies a redefinition of what the law considers to be public and private. Prior to the 1993 World Human Rights Conference, it was not recognized that this type of violence was a violation of human rights, which left the field wide open for impunity within private family interactions regarding threats to human dignity.

Traditional civil law on marriage is not sufficient to resolve conflicts within interpersonal relations, because it does not recognize the violent potential of day-to-day family conflicts. Thus women's groups, in partnership with progressive legislators, have lobbied for a series of laws, some already enacted, to put an end to the sufferings caused by violence within households. There are, at this writing, specific laws on domestic violence in Puerto Rico, Peru, Chile, Argentina and recently in Ecuador.

The inadequacy of criminal laws regarding domestic violence is well-known, especially in Ecuador, which forbids spouses to denounce each other (Art. 28 of the Code of Civil Procedures). Discussion of the relevance of classing domestic abuse under criminal law does not mean that criminal behaviour within affective family relations should not be punished more drastically. The difficulty lies in the move to prevent the criminal-law system from becoming involved, for the sake of an ideal of family stability. This means that the state provides no protection for other family forms, such as female-headed households. Manifestations of intra-family violence must be appreciated according to their seriousness, and criminal-law coercion must be used when appropriate in dealing with crimes occurring within homes.

One possibility for regulation would be to *define the crime of abuse within intra-family relations,* in order to distinguish it from the crime of injuries, which is of a more general nature. One advantage of such a description would be to include a definition of physical, psychic and sexual violence, as outlined in the Inter-American Convention to Prevent, Punish and Eradicate Violence against Women. This legislation would complement specific legislation of a civil nature, which is applied to the less serious modes of domestic violence.

The other possibility, being applied at present in a number of Latin American countries (Peru, Chile, Argentina and Ecuador), is to have specific civil laws that charge judges with passing cases over to criminal courts when crimes have apparently been committed.[11] The same mode is applied, even if there is no specific law, in the other countries, because all bodies of law have constitutional provisions protecting personal security and criminal-law codes define the crime of injury. The difficulty under this mode is that the crime of injury does not recognize psychic violence, and many measure the seriousness of the action in terms of the days of lost work, which is an inadequate measurement of domestic violence.

Protection for Women in Prostitution

The notion of chastity is used in criminal-law codes to discriminate against women involved in sexual trade, based on the doctrine that women who are prostitutes are not "chaste." This position violates international human-rights standards. Therefore, laws that reduce penalties when victims are prostitutes, as in Venezuela, El Salvador, and Paraguay, must be repealed.

Criminal-law protection must also be expanded to prevent traffic in women, in order to safeguard their fundamental rights, which are seriously limited due to the lack of effective legal resources on the national and international level. The Fourth World Conference on Women Platform for Action obliges states to penalize those involved in international networks for sexual exploitation (No. 230 n.).

Greater Guarantees for the Enforcement of Support Obligations

Women are poorly protected from failure to comply with the obligation to provide family support. Criminal-law provisions regarding alimony, child support and so on are too broad and full of loopholes. The requirement to exhaust possibilities of a civil lawsuit for alimony in some legal systems, and the possibility of excusing an irresponsible father because he does not have the money, makes it impossible for mothers to make claims. This lack of support may jeopardize children's lives in situations of extreme poverty, but also undermines family ties and reduces family security in all classes.

It is fundamental to guarantee, even by criminal sanctions, conditions whereby both parents equitably assume the responsibility for their children's care and protection. Many restrictions on women's professional and working lives originate in paternal irresponsibility.

These proposals are intended to provide guidance in detecting the most flagrant discriminatory measures, and to convince the broadest possible sectors to spare no efforts in getting them repealed or amended, as the case may be. Justice must be given yet another chance to adapt, change, and respond to the expectations of a significant number of female citizens. Justice is undergoing critical evaluation in all Latin American countries, and requires opportunities to become legitimate. These guidelines are intended to offer just such an opportunity. Action upon them is therefore urgent—not only for women, but for all of society.   ❖

Notes

1. Argentina, Brazil, Bolivia, Cuba, Chile, Colombia, Costa Rica, Ecuador, El Salvador, Guatemala, Honduras, Nicaragua, Mexico, Paraguay, Panama, Peru, Dominican Republic, Uruguay and Venezuela.

2. The preparatory process prior to the World Conference on Human Rights fostered challenges to the traditional human rights doctrine on the basis of women's experience. In Latin America, the "Our Agenda" Satellite Meeting drew up a list of proposals to guide the work of Latin American groups at the conference (Assessment and Strategies about Women's Human Rights in Latin America and the Caribbean. San José, Costa Rica, 3-5 December 1992) and the "Among Women" Network formed National Committees in various countries to prepare assessments of women's human rights status (Women and Human Rights in Latin America, November 1993).

3. The Platform for Action that emerged from the Fourth World Conference on Women (1995) states that governments must rework national laws and legal practice in the areas of family, civil, criminal, labor and business law to ensure implementation of the principles of international human rights instruments, repeal those laws containing sex-based discrimination, and remove gender prejudice from the administration of justice (Art. 232d). In the chapter on Women and Health, the Platform postulates that governments must provide treatment for injury due to illegal abortion and must review legislation containing punitive measures against women who have undergone illegal abortions (Art. 107 l.)

4. Male hormonal changes have not been so widely researched, much less subjected to public reflection; indeed, it is believed that males are "invulnerable" to any such change.

5. If the woman consents to abortion, the code establishes a penalty of 1 to 4 years in prison; if she waits for the child to be born, the penalty is 1 to 3 years; if she has the child, fails to register the birth, and abandons it before it is three days old, the penalty is significantly reduced (up to 50% in some cases).

6. When this document was published in Spanish, this provision also existed in the Peruvian criminal code. Since its publication, however, protest by women's groups has resulted in its repeal.

7. Guadalupe León (1995) for example, documents the run-around women get in police and judicial institutions in Ecuador.

8. Often such norms are unconstitutional, as the constitutional principle of equality overrides discriminatory criminal law norms (Prieto 1994).

9. It is important to regulate the performance of authorized abortions in public hospitals, as done in Cuba and Panama. Otherwise, clandestine abortions will continue, with serious consequences for women's lives and health (Hurtado Pozo 1982: 178).

10. Brazil's National Council of Women's Rights has studied some lawsuits in which the victims were women, including two cases of homicide, in which the defense argued that the aggressions leading to death were grounded in the "defense of honor" (Conselho Nacional dos Direitos da Mulher 1987).

11. Ecuador should rework its provisions that are incompatible with the spirit of the law of 12 December 1995, as proposed in the Draft Law regarding Violence Against Women and Families.

References

Bustos Ramírez, Juan (1986). *Manual de Derecho Penal Español.* Barcelona: Editorial Ariel.

Instituto de Estudios de la Mujer (CEMUJER) (1995). "Norma Virginia Guirola de Herrera (CEMUJER). "Propuestas de Reformas al Proyecto de Código Penal," mimeo, San Salvador.

Chejter, Silvia (1990). *La voz tutelada. Violación y Voyeurismo.* Montevideo, Uruguay: Editorial Nordan-Comunidad.

Conselho de Direitos de la Mulher (1987). *Cuando a vitima e mulher.* Brasilia: Ministry of Justice.

Hurtado Pozo, José (1982). *Manual de Derecho Penal. Part I: Homicido y Aborto.* Lima.

Jelin, Elizabeth (1993). *Ante, de, en, y? Mujeres, Derechos Humanos Entre Mujeres.* Lima.

Lagarde, Marcel (1996). *Identidad de género y Derechos Humanos en Estudios Básicos de Derechos Humanos IV. IIDH Serie Estudios de Derechos Humanos* , Vol.4 Instituto Interamericano de Derechos Humanos (IIDH). San José, Costa Rica.

Laqueur, Thomas (1990). *La construcción del sexo. Cuerpo y Género desde los griegos hasta Freud.* Madrid: Ediciones Cátedra.

Leon, Guadalupe (1985). *Del Encubrimiento a la Impunidad. Diagnóstico sobre la violencia de género. Ecuador,* 1989-1995. Quito, Ecuador: DEIME Ediciones.

Navarro, Milagro (1992). *La Mujer en los hechos y el Derecho.* Cordoba, Argentina: Advocatus.

Plata, María Isabel (1995). "Los nuevos derechos: el reconocimiento de los derechos sexuales y reproductivos." Seminar on Human Rights with a Gender Perspective. National University of Colombia, 30-31 October.

Pateman, Carole (1989). *The Disorder of Women: Democracy, Feminism and Political Theory.* Stanford, CA: Stanford University Press.

Prieto, Esther (1994). *Mujer y Justicia Penal.* Asunción: Centro de Estudios Humanitarios.

Siles Vallejos, Abraham (1995). "Con el sólo dicho de la agraviada. Es discriminatoria la justicia en procesos por violación sexual de mujeres?" DEMUS, Estudio para la Defensa de los Derechos de la Mujer, Lima, Peru.

Soto Cabrera, Tatiana (1988). "Los mecanismos legales desprotectores de la víctima de agresión sexual." Graduate thesis, University of Costa Rica, San José, Costa Rica.

List of Criminal Law Codes

Código Penal de la Nación Argentina, 17th ed., Editorial Abedelo-Perrot, Buenos Aires, 1984

Código Penal República de Bolivia, Editorial Serrano, Cochabamba, 1992

Código Penal del Brasil del año 1993

Código Penal de la República de Colombia, Los Códigos Penales Iberoamericans, Ediciones Forum Pacis, Bogotá, 1994

Código de la República de Costa Rica, Los Códigos Penales Iberoamericans, Ediciones Forum Pacis, Bogotá, 1994

Código Penal de la República de Cuba, Los Códigos Penales Iberoamericans, Ediciones Forum Pacis, Bogotá, 1994

Código Penal de la República de Chile, Edición Jurídica de Chile, Santiago, 1992

Código Penal de la República de Ecuador, Corporación de Estudios y Publicaciones, 1994

Código Penal de la República de Guatemala, Cuarta Edición, 1975

Código Penal de la República de Honduras, Graficentro Editores, Tegucigalpa, 1993

Código Penal para el Distrito Federal, Los Códigos Penales Iberoamericans, Ediciones Forum Pacis, Bogotá, 1994

Código Penal de la República de Nicaragua, La Gaceta, Diario Oficial, Managua 1992

Código Penal de la República de Panamá, 6th ed., Editorial Mizrachi & Pujol, 1993

Código Penal de la República de Paraguay, Colección Legislación Paraguaya, Edición 1995

Código Penal de la República del Perú, Edición no Oficial, Lima, 1991

Código Penal de la República Dominicana, Editorial Tiempo, Santo Domingo, 1992

Código Penal de la República de El Salvador, Diario Oficial #63, bk. 238, San Salvador, 1973

Código Penal de la República Oriental del Uruguay, 2nd ed., Ediciones Jurídicas Amalio M. Fernández, Montevideo, 1978

Código Penal de la República de Venezuela, Gaceta Oficial #915, Caracas, 1964

Combatting Violence Against Women in the Caribbean

ROBERTA CLARKE

"Our societies are organised around hierarchical power relations
with male domination which reduces women
to economic and emotional dependency."

Gender-based violence or the threat of it is a social problem which takes many forms depending on the cultural context: from domestic abuse to forced prostitution; from dowry deaths to sexual harassment; from rape to involuntary sterilisation. Violence or its threat shapes the contours of every woman's life; it confines where she goes and what she does, limiting her freedom of movement, speech, and assembly, and undermining her sense of personhood, her human dignity, and her rights in the world. While all individuals are vulnerable to violence, this risk and accordingly, the experience of violence is gendered. Men and women suffer difference consequences, according to their gender. Moreover, whether the victim is male or female, the perpetrator is almost always male. And frequently, the perpetrator is motivated by issues of gender, such as the need to assert male power.

Women are most vulnerable to the consequences of a gender ideology that subordinates women at the level of the family. The family socialises its members to accept gender inequality, which finds expression in the unequal division of labour and power over resources. A potent weapon in this socialisation process is the use of violence against women.

The history of the Caribbean is replete with violation and subordination, stemming from the experience of slavery and colonialism. But only recently has the typology of violence in the region included gender violence, including domestic violence; historical work documents how rape

---

This article is an abbreviated version of a much longer report prepared by the UNIFEM Caribbean Office and published under the title "Violence Against Women in the Caribbean: State and Non-State Responses."

and other forms of violence were used to control women in the post-emancipation 19th and 20th centuries as women attempted to define their own lives (Reddock 1994).

Throughout the Caribbean, accurate estimates of the extent violence against women are hard to obtain, owing to the insensitivity of police and other authorities and consequent widespread failure to report sexual offences. Yet statistics complied by courts, crisis centres and police stations confirm well-known anecdotal and experiential evidence. In most countries, the greatest threat to women is from their families and partners, most of it occurring in their homes. In Guyana, a 1989 study revealed that two out of three women in conjugal unions had been beaten at least once by their partners and a full third of these regularly (Danns and Persad 1989). In Suriname, a 1993 pilot study indicates that one in three women in unions have experienced domestic violence, while one in five complaints to police stations are women victims of violence (CAFRA 1993). And in Trinidad and Tobago between October 1991 and April 1994, a total of 8,297 applications for protection orders were made, largely by women (Creque 1995).

Crisis centre statistics show women reporting domestic abuse in greater numbers. Reports in Jamaica increased from 414 in 1985 to 2176 in 1991 (Jamaica National Preparatory Committee 1995); while those in St. Lucia increased from five in 1988 to 429 in 1993 (Fletcher-Paul 1994); in Anguilla reports went from 37 during 1985-87 to 317 during 1991-93; in Bahamas they increased from 150 in 1985-87 to 436 in 1991-93. In Trinidad and Tobago, where the police recorded 1517 complaints of domestic violence in 1991 and 1444 in 1993, 46 percent of the cases concerned physical abuse, while 23 percent concerned sexual abuse, rape, and other sexual offences (Creque 1995).

Statistics on rape, while notoriously unreliable as an indicator of this type of violence, still provide some indication of the risk of being female: in the Dominican Republic it is reported that one sexual violation occurs every eight hours; in Trinidad and Tobago, according to police statistics, a woman is raped every 1.75 days. In Jamaica, where there were 1297 reported cases of rape and carnal abuse in 1993, 38 percent of the victims were between the ages of 18 and 25, while 44 percent were girls under 16. That year too, 52 juvenile boys appeared before the court on rape and other sexual offence charges (Annual Statistical Reports 1993).

In terms of the administration of justice, what is noticeable from the statistics is the relatively low number of charges and prosecutions, and even lower number of convictions, in relation to the number of reports. Reasons for this include victim reluctance to press charges, police inaction, evidential difficulties, and court backlog. Violence against women is frequently rendered invisible.

In most countries, the family is supposed to cope with such problems internally, making it hard to enlist outside help, a problem made worse by the tendency for authorities to trivialize the issue and its impact. In general, throughout the region, there are no protocols set up for police treatment of domestic violence cases which would demand mandatory investigation and data compilation. Even at health institutions, while records note causes of admission, the information is not disaggregated by sex nor often by cause of injury.

As a result of increased international attention, however, gender-specific violence has become a human-rights issue in the region. In 1993, at the World Conference on Human Rights in Vienna, state parties accepted that gender-based violence and all forms of sexual harassment and exploitation, including those resulting from cultural biases, are incompatible with the dignity and worth of the human person and must be eliminated. Following this, the UN General Assembly adopted the Declaration on the Elimination of Violence Against Women, which defines violence against women as "any act of gender-based violence that results in, or is likely to result in, physical, sexual, or psychological harm or suffering to women, including threats of such acts." Soon thereafter, in June 1994, the Inter-American Convention on the Prevention, Punishment, and Eradication of Violence (Belem Convention), which defines violence in both the public and private spheres, was adopted by the Organization of American States (OAS).

While the UN Declaration does not place any binding obligations on states to comply, nor does it provide mechanisms for reporting on state action, the Belem Convention includes such mechanisms, mandating information or measures adopted to prevent violence against women in national reports to the Inter-American Commission of Women. The OAS Convention also provides that states may request of the Inter-American Court of Human Rights advisory opinions on the interpretation of the convention and allows petitions to the Inter-American Commission that contain denunciations or complaints of violations which shall be considered in accordance with procedures established by the American Convention on Human Rights.

At the national level, similar gains can be seen in the recognition of violence against women as a public political issue, one that demands state action. Responses by both governments and non-governmental organizations (NGOs) include legal measures as well as efforts to establish family courts staffed by trained judiciary and supported by social services. Throughout the region, women's organisations have called for systematic training and education of the police as part of basic training. In many countries NGOs have responded to violence against women by setting up crisis centres, shelters, legal aid clinics, education programmes in schools and communities, and media watches.

Sexual Offences

While in all countries of the region sexual offences against women, including rape or carnal knowledge of female children, are criminal offences, for most, the old English law on rape continues in force. In Belize, Grenada, and St. Lucia, where criminal law has been codified, the codes restate the old English rules. Thus rape under common law is defined as sexual intercourse by a male with a female who is not his wife without her consent, or with consent extorted by threats of bodily harm, impersonating her husband, or by false representations of the nature and quality of the act. The crime is punishable by prison terms ranging from a few years to life imprisonment.

In Anguilla, Belize, Dominica, Grenada, Guyana, Jamaica, St. Christopher and Nevis, St. Lucia, St. Vincent and the Grenadines it is an offence for a man to have sexual intercourse with a woman whom he knows to be his granddaughter, daughter, sister, or mother, though prison terms for convicted offenders vary among countries. There is no legislation in Antigua which specifically provides for the offence of incest. Recent legislation in the Bahamas, Barbados and Trinidad and Tobago, recognizing the particularities of the family in the region, have also made it a criminal offence, akin to incest, for an adult to have sexual intercourse with a minor when the minor is the adult's adopted child, stepchild, ward, or dependent.

In the Caribbean as elsewhere, women are discouraged from bringing charges of sexual offences by a number of features of the law, notably the absenceof an all-embracing criminalisation of forced or coerced sexual intercourse within marriage, the need for corroboration in order to prove lack of consent; allowing evidence of the victim's sexual history; the need to provide immediate evidence; as well as the trauma of public court procedures. In response, the CARICOM Secretariat has developed model legislation concerning sexual offences and amended legislation exists in the

Bahamas, Barbados, and Trinidad and Tobago. The age of consent for women is 14.

While in Barbados corroboration is no longer needed for a conviction, the common law requirement to warn against conviction in the absence of corroboration was not abolished in either the Bahamas or Trinidad and Tobago. Even after reforms the underlying assumption that women fabricate rape testimony continues to pervade the administration of justice. Moreover, under common law, the law considers the victim's past sexual history relevant to the question of consent—the assumption being that someone who has been sexually active is more likely to consent. As a result, cross-examination allows extensive questions about the victim's social and sexual life with the view to denigrating her character. While both Barbados and the Bahamas now exclude such evidence, in Trinidad and Tobago the court has discretion to allow such evidence upon application of the accused.

The rule requiring the victim to provide evidence of a fresh or recent complaint has been abolished in Trinidad and Tobago, which recognizes that for a variety of social and psychological reasons, women delay bringing sexual assault complaints. Barbados requires the judge to warn the jury that a delay does not necessarily indicate that the allegation is false. Owing to the fact that court proceedings can exacerbate the victim's trauma, Barbados, Grenada, St. Christopher and Nevis, and Trinidad and Tobago provide for anonymity of both victim and accused and Trinidad and Tobago also allow *in camera* hearings for sexual offence cases, as do Anguilla, St. Christopher and Nevis, and Guyana. In Barbados, in camera hearings are permitted only when the complainant is a minor.

Domestic Violence
Women have made considerable gains in getting legislation to address domestic violence since the mid-1980s, including protection orders. The Bahamas, Barbados, Belize, Grenada, Jamaica, St. Lucia, St. Vincent and the Grenadines, Trinidad and Tobago now focus on extending protection to battered women and similar legislation is now consideration in Guyana. In most countries there has also been considerable debate about the suitability of the criminal justice system to manage the problem of domestic violence. While some argue the desirability of arrest, prosecution and sentencing, others insist that the appropriate response should emphasize rehabilitation, mediation, and conciliation. In those countries which have recently enacted legislation, a middle way was sought, following the CARICOM model, which increases available options by enabling a victim, whether spouse

(which in all countries but the Bahamas includes common-law spouse) or children of spouse, to seek a protection order at the same time as she decides whether to file a criminal complaint. This approach is predicated on the belief that battered women are more immediately concerned with securing refuge and safety than with prosecution, a belief supported by the experience of organisations that work with battered women as well as by women's reluctance to press criminal charges against their batterers. In Guyana, where the only study of women's responses to domestic violence has been done, it was found that only 6 percent of victims went to the police for help and protection while 62 percent sought help in their kinship networks (Danns and Parsad 1989).

Legislation provides that a victim of domestic violence may seek a protection order where a spouse or former spouse, parent, or other member of the household has engaged in conduct of a violent nature, has threatened such behaviour, or has behaved in a harassing and offensive way. In Trinidad and Tobago and Belize, "offensive or harassing behaviour" includes abusive and threatening language, malicious property damage, and threats of physical violence, while in Trinidad and Tobago it also includes stalking behaviour and wilful neglect of a dependent.

In case of harassment, however, applicants must show that this conduct was sufficient to cause fear for their safety. In all domestic violence legislation, provision is also made for counselling; in Belize and Barbados, counselling is mandatory. In Barbados, one of the factors which the court is obliged to take into account in considering applications for protection orders is the preservation and protection of the institution of marriage and the family as the fundamental unit of society.

Legislation regarding domestic violence also makes access to the courts swift and effective, including mandatory hearings within a short time of application; personal service orders; the power to grant interim protection orders; *in camera* proceedings, anonymity of parties. Most of the new laws also empower the police to make an arrest without a warrant in cases of breach of protection orders.

While evaluation of the impact of the new legislation has been limited, evidence from Trinidad and Tobago suggests an overwhelming use of the provisions by women. Anecdotal evidence indicates that legal proceedings are still agonisingly slow for women in crisis and that the judiciary, lawyers, and police must be continually challenged to fight the causes and not only the symptoms of violence against women.

While in countries with no specific domestic violence legislation, victims of domestic violence are still able to bring civil action against the person who assaults her, in practice, the legal costs of a civil action effectively prohibit the majority of poor and unemployed women from seeking redress. In addition, in all CARICOM countries and in the Netherlands Antilles, assault, wounding, and other violence offences against the person are subject to criminal penalty as well. In Antigua, the Bahamas, Barbados, British Virgin Islands, Dominica, Jamaica, Montserrat, St. Christopher and Nevis, St. Lucia, Trinidad and Tobago, where a person is convicted of aggravated assault upon a child, the offender can be fined or imprisoned in excess of that allowed for a common assault.

Sexual Harassment

Within the CARICOM Caribbean, only the Bahamas has legislation prohibiting sexual harassment in the workplace. The Sexual Offences and Domestic Violence Act of the Bahamas makes it a criminal offence punishable by a fine of $5000 and/or imprisonment for a maximum of two years. The offence applies to the solicitation of sexual favours by a prospective employer, employer or co-worker by the promise or the threat of any favour, benefit, advantage or disadvantage and when advantages are sought by the promise of sexual favours. Unfortunately there is no remedy, such as reinstatement, for those unfairly dismissed as a result of resistance to sexual harassment.

Other Responses

In practically all Caribbean countries, even those with new legislation regarding sexual offences and domestic violence, implementation of the law has been hampered by the dominant cultural attitudes shared by those within the justice system, especially the police. Effective response to violence against women demands an understanding of the dynamics of violence, consistent treatment of offenders, and provision of services to the victims and their families. As a result, there is growing support for the establishment of family courts, staffed by trained judiciary and supported by social services. Family courts exist in Jamaica, Belize, Grenada, and St. Vincent and the Grenadines, dealing with child custody and maintenance; guardianship and matrimonial proceedings, and in Belize, also domestic violence cases. Family courts are being considered in Antigua and in Trinidad and Tobago.

In all countries in the region, police officers receive little training in the law and practice relating to violence against women, and it is only in Jamaica, Trinidad and Tobago and St. Christopher and Nevis that specific units have been established with the police with a specific mandate regarding violence against women. In Trinidad and Tobago, the Juvenile Bureau and Counselling unit within the police department handles cases of rape, abuse and incest, and is also engaged in educational outreach to schools. The unit however, is badly understaffed, and lacks offices outside the capital city of Port of Spain. A similar unit, the Delinquency Unit, in St. Christopher and Nevis deals with cases of domestic violence, child abuse, and problematic children, to provide counselling and liaise with other government departments, In Jamaica, investigative units for sexual offences have been set up in each parish in order to intervene in cases of sexual offence and secure counselling and medical treatment. These units also conduct education programmes in schools, churches, and community groups. Barbados, which lacks specialised units, police policy mandates quick response to complaints of sexual violence and the police force has had training seminars on methods of investigation of such offences, as has St. Vincent and the Grenadines and Guyana.

Beyond this, however, there is little to prevent the problem of gender violence. None of the governments in the region operate transition housing, though Trinidad and Tobago subsidizes the operation of shelters, and few engage in sustained education programmes on the issue. Where such initiatives exist, they are undertaken by Women's Affairs departments. Thus training courses and manuals as well as public awareness courses have been developed in Guyana, Antigua and Belize, while in Dominica the Women's Bureau offers counselling to women on a daily basis and provides monetary support to help them overcome the dependency syndrome which so often aggravates, if not directly causes, domestic abuse.

NGO responses, as mentioned, include setting up crisis centres, shelters, legal aid clinics, and education programmes to assist victims of abuse. Hot lines for rape victims of victims of violence are operative in Barbados, Belize, Dominica, Grenada; while crisis centres, offering counselling and often shelter, exist in the Bahamas, Jamaica, Guyana, St. Lucia and Trinidad and Tobago. In almost every country there are also women's media watches, resources and referral centres and various legal aid services.

Conclusions and Recommendations

Because law is not a neutral force in society, the transformation of laws related to violence against women has had a powerful effect on consciousness of women's rights and security and protection by the law. Perhaps even more than regulating behaviour it is symbolic of the ethics and norms of society. In forcing governments to enact these laws, women's organisations have brought about a recognition that violence against women is a political issue, not a cultural or private one. They have made the point that where acts by persons which violate women's rights to personal security can be linked to systemic or structural inequality, then the state has a responsibility to endeavour to prevent these violations and in effect to respond to them.

Notwithstanding the legislative gains, all countries require more integrated and comprehensive responses to violence against women. Strategies to combat violence must include provisions of services for the victim as well as action to bring about the elimination of inequality between men and women. For despite all the initiatives, it is evident that violence against women is increasing, not decreasing. Rigourous research is needed to document these trends.

Explaining gender violence in terms of hierarchical gender relations risks oversimplification in terms of responses. The nuances of this violence must be elaborated if effective programmes and services are to be established. For example, in Trinidad and Tobago it is reported that over two-thirds of the domestic-violence offenders who appear in court are alcoholics or drug addicts, many of them also living in poverty. And in the only study of its kind to date, research from Guyana shows that although abuse occurs in all income groups, poor women experience the most frequent and violent forms of abuse. Further research would indicate whether there are predictors of violence in each cultural context which render women more or less vulnerable.

The connection between masculine stereotypes and the culture of violence must also be explored. Male violence is increasing in the Caribbean as it is in other areas. Violence against women, while pervasive, is one aspect of male violence. The centrality of gender to the understanding of violence necessitates an examination of the ways in which societies socialize and also reproduce behaviours and norms which are conducive to violence. Society also reproduces violence through the criminal justice system itself, which must be reviewed accordingly.

Any attempt to resolve the problem of violence against women must also take account of those whose efforts to leave situations of violence are severely impaired by poverty. Women with few resources have few options; thus while violence against women occurs in all classes, in all regions, it is indisputable that the economic crisis in the Caribbean region reduces poor women's power to resist. Thus in developing programmes to combat violence against women recognition of the ways in which cultural, economic and social factors reinforce each other and the need for multi-focused approaches, including ways to ensure women's equal participation in policy formulation, decision-making and development, are critical.

Over the last five years a number of recommendations have focuses on increasing legal response, education and training, research and data, and services for victims. As regards legal reform the CARICOM model legislation on domestic violence, sexual offence and sexual harassment in the workplace should be followed by all countries in the region. This must be accompanied by reform in the administration of justice, particularly through training that draws on the relationship between gender discrimination and violence against women. Fundamental principles upon which training should be based are as follows:

- Women have a fundamental right to be free from all forms of violence and fear of violence against them;
- the responsibility for violence acts against women rests with the perpetrators, and social policy and practice should reflect this;
- intervention by the justice system should be empowering to women rather than acting to perpetuate their oppression.

States should promote the training of key groups, such as judges, magistrates, lawyers, health professionals and teachers, and include knowledge of services available.

Women's organizations have been in the forefront of action to eliminate violence as well as to provide services to victims of violence against women. They therefore must develop minimum standards for state treatment of the issue, which can be used to advocate for legislative and aministrative reforms. Yet while women avail themselves of the legislation where it exists, they are also quickly exhausted by the legal process and disillusioned by the lack of state capacity or willingness to protect them once an injunction has been granted. Governments, under pressure from the IMF and World

Bank, are cutting back on spending for social services, leaving the NGOs to weave and carry the "safety net"; thus shelters and crisis centres are badly in need of money and other resources at a time when demand for them is increasing daily. In this context, women's organisations must call on governments to take on the provision of such services.

Effective policy development must also be informed by reliable data on the incidence of violence against women, women's responses to violence, and their need for services. Women's organizations and human-rights organizations should collaborate and work with governments in the development of education and consciousness-raising programmes emphasising that violence against women is a violation of women's human rights and monitoring state action in eliminating such violence.

Violence against women is not a women's problem; it is a social problem—and thus a social responsibility. Only when this fact is recognized by both men and women will we be able to pressure governments successfully to take on their responsibilities to half of their citizens.   ❖

References

Creque, M. (1995). *A Study of the Incidence of Domestic Violence in Trinidad and Tobago from 1991 to 1993*. Port of Spain: Shelter for Battered Women and Trinidad and Tobago Coalition Against Domestic Violence.

Danns, G. and B. Shiw Parsad (1989). "Domestic Violence and Marital Relationships in the Caribbean. A Guyanese Case Study." Women's Studies Unit, University of Guyana.

Fletcher-Paul, L.(1994). *St. Lucia National Report on the Status of Women*. St. Lucia: Ministry of Legal Affairs.

Government of Jamaica (1993). *Annual Statistical Reports 1993*. Kingston.

Pargass, G. (1991). "The Incidence of Sexual Offences in the Caribbean." Paper presented at the CAFRA/UNECLAC Meeting on Women, Violence and the Law, Trinidad and Tobago.

Reddock, Rhoda (1994). *Women, Labour and Politics in Trinidad and Tobago: A History.* London: Zed Books, 1994

United Nations 1993. *Report of the Expert Group Meeting on Violence Against Women*. New York: UN Secretariat.

List of Legislation

Barbados Sexual Offences Act, 1991

Barbados Domestic Violence Act, 1992

Bahamas Sexual Offences and Domestic Violence Act, 1991

Belize Domestic Violence Act, 1993

Jamaica Domestic Violence Act, 1995

St. Lucia Domestic Violence Act, 1995

St. Vincent and the Grenadines Domestic Violence Act, 1994

Trinidad and Tobago Sexual Offences Act, 1986

Trinidad and Tobago Domestic Violence Act

The Laws of Belize

Grenada Criminal Code

Guyana Criminal Law

St. Lucia Criminal Code

St. Vincent and the Grenadines Criminal Code

Revised Laws of Antigua 1992

Revised Laws of British Virgin Islands 1991

Revised Laws of Montserrat 1965

Revised Laws of Dominica 1990

Unequal Status, Unequal Development: Gender Violence in Mexico

PATRICIA DUARTE SÁNCHEZ AND GERARDO GONZÁLEZ

*"For feminists, it is important to give our work against gender violence
a new perspective, incorporating it into the national discussion
of democracy. To do this, we need to reframe our discussion of
gender violence within the concept of citizenship,
rather than relegating it to a struggle between men and women."*

Throughout the world, in virtually every society, the marginalization of women is perpetuated over generations, reflected in a complex pattern of discrimination and violence that pervades women's lives, both public and private. In Latin America and the Caribbean, feminists have worked for over 20 years to expose and prevent gender violence, most recently through the effort to broaden the concept of human rights to include the right to be free of violence. In Mexico, as elsewhere, women's groups have struggled to make the issue of violence against women a cornerstone of the national human development agenda.

The feminist movement in Mexico began speaking out against rape in 1975, calling public attention to a social problem which until then had not been made visible. Since then, a lot of ground has been covered: women have organized in non-governmental organizations (NGOs) throughout the country, extending services to survivors of domestic violence as well as rape—including medical treatment, counselling, and legal representation. They have succeeded in getting legislation outlawing gender violence, first proposed more than 50 years before, reintroduced in the national assembly. Since the late 1980s, feminists have concentrated less on opposing government policy and more on complementing it—with advocacy and public education campaigns—in an effort to get beyond individual treatment to collective prevention.

During that time, service programmes have been created in a number of different public institutions, specialized public agencies have been set up to address these issues, and centres have been established to provide therapy for victims and to offer education and assistance in dealing with intra-family violence. In addition, legal reforms have changed the ways in which sex crimes are treated in the courts.

In addition to providing services and engaging in the legal reform process, feminists have also managed to involve the government and broad sectors of the population in a wider discussion of gender relations. Today, as a result of all these efforts, gender violence is no longer confined to the private sphere; it is a public issue that is debated in academia, in labour unions and political parties, in grassroots organizations, in the urban movement and in professional schools. It is included in the stated policy of the public health sector, the Ministry of Foreign Relations, the Ministry of Public Education, and the Ministry of the Interior, as well as in human-rights organizations and some Attorney Generals' offices; it is also included in national programmes charged with working for the welfare of children and the family (the National System for the Integral Development of the Family, or DIF).

As a result, social images have been greatly transformed: ordinary people have changed their vision of rape victims, abandoning the widely held view that the woman is somehow to blame, that her looks or behaviour had in some way "provoked" the violence. Opinions toward the aggressor have also changed; the "medical" or "clinical" view of a rapist as someone who is "mentally ill" is now rare, and receives little support in academic or popular discourse.

Nowhere is the change more evident than in the Mexican legal system: not only are laws more effective in discouraging gender violence, they also challenge the view of violence as an accepted method for solving differences between men and women. In the revised Penal Code, issued in 1991, the term "sex crimes" was changed to "crimes against liberty and normal psycho-sexual development," the concept of copulation was defined to be more inclusive, and the designation "crimes against modesty" was changed to "sexual abuse." Such atavistic concepts as "chastity and honour" were removed from the definition of statutory rape, and the provision allowing an aggressor to obtain a pardon by marrying his victim was eliminated from the law. Also eliminated was the crime of "abduction," in a recognition of the erotic/sexual assumptions implicit in distinguishing this from other kinds of kidnapping. And, for the first time in Mexico, sexual harassment was defined as a crime.

Despite this progress, the experience of the last 10 years has made it clear that a much more extensive series of transformations are needed to change the condition of structural vulnerability which currently characterizes the lives of Mexican women and children. Although the laws look good on paper, there is no national system to make a record of these crimes, and a lack of institutional coordination (among Attorney Generals' offices, educational institutions, health services, family services, etc.) is common. No study has yet been undertaken to try to assess the extent of the problem. Moreover, the Specialized Agencies for Sex Crimes lack standardized criteria and are hampered by a bureaucratic dependency on various regional authorities; there is no centralization in the investigation of criminals with a regular pattern of behaviour. Training for law and social service agency officials includes technical education but neglects the human aspects which could help change attitudes of public officials, provide victims with integrated assistance and demystify the problem of crimes of gender violence. Currently women must face the costs of the violence they suffer alone; it is practically unheard of for victims of gender violence to receive economic compensation.

Legal reforms are also needed in order for legislators to recognize intra-family violence as an issue that is fundamentally different from aggression occurring outside the ome or in public social situations. The legal system currently addresses these kinds of violence without distinction under the generic classification of "crimes of bodily harm." Also needed are public policies designed to incorporate large sectors of the community into efforts to prevent violence.

For feminists, it is important to give our work against gender violence a new perspective, incorporating it into the national discussion of democracy. To do this, we need to reframe our discussion of gender violence within the concept of citizenship, rather than relegating it to a struggle between men and women.

When we speak of the causes and effects of a phenomenon such as gender violence, we cannot and should not draw narrowly defined conclusions or offer single-cause analyses to defend our theories. A glance at the literature on this issue shows the widespread prevalence of such over-generalized concepts as "profiles of rapists," "post-traumatic syndromes," "profiles of rape victims," "formulas for the prevention of violence," and so on, as if there were some sort of standardized diagnostic recipe for this complex phenomenon.

The experience of people working with those, primarily women, who have been victims of gender violence is that the recipe changes constantly, according to such factors as class, education, emotional condition when the violence occurred, age, knowledge about gender violence, physical health, life history and even the victim's culture. This experience suggests that to prevent gender violence, it is necessary to open new ways of understanding, to ascribe new meanings to the ways in which the phenomenon is interpreted, to create the conditions necessary for a new level of reflection (both our own reflection and reflection by victims of gender violence) about what happened and its consequences.

In this regard it is import to remember that theories are only the tools that we use, according to our ability, to prevent gender violence, assist victims, offer therapy or create national programmes; the level at which we work is less important than the awareness that no level of work can be totally judgement-free. Changing a "social image" involves the social perspective, but it also involves the political perspective, the structural transformation of women's condition, and therefore it also involves changing myths in order to establish what U.S. anthropologist Margaret Mead called the new taboos appropriate to the society which we are working to create.

Rape Crisis Brochures: A COVAC Study

UNIFEM, through its programme on the elimination of violence against women, has supported the Mexican Collective to Fight Violence Against Women (COVAC), which focuses mainly on the issues of rape, domestic violence and the sexual abuse of children, with emphasis on training, research, dissemination of information, assistance to victims and lobbying for improved legislation. COVAC has also been involved in defining the position of the feminist movement at the national and regional levels concerning gender violence. With UNIFEM's support, COVAC has recently reevaluated its work at the grassroots level, analyzing the last 15 years of work by NGOs against gender violence in Mexico.

In 1996 COVAC conducted an analysis of 25 rape-prevention brochures published in Spanish by NGOs, private institutions and government agencies in Mexico, Latin America and the United States. While not pretending to be comprehensive, the study was nevertheless revealing. First, it showed that despite very different perspectives, in all of these brochures the way in which the problem of women and violence is presented rests on the assumption that such violence is natural, a consequence of biology or nature, and thus inevitable. Thus, when offering advice on prevention, 19 brochures (76%) gave advice to the individual—about how to dress, how to walk, when to go out and with whom, so as not to provoke violence—while only six (24%) mentioned collective approaches, drawing on legal or social sanctions to denounce the violence itself. In so doing the brochures reinforce the idea that violence is an individual problem rather than a social one, and that the behaviour of the individual should change rather than that of the aggressor.

Second, the study showed an assumption and identification with the idea that being raped is the worst thing that can happen to a woman, rather than conceiving of the phenomenon as an accident occurring in people's lives without their wanting it or doing anything to make it happen. Thus only six of the brochures give a positive message to women—offering other possible responses, such as seizing happiness and vitality, carrying on one's life with dignity, in spite of the violence. In contrast, nine offered no message at all to women, while ten promoted highly rhetorical responses, such as all men are potential aggressors, or, by denouncing violence we are free of violence.

The experience of everyone who has worked in this field, however, makes clear that violence prevention cannot be accomplished quickly, or by single individuals; it takes structural transformation. What is needed is a social climate that respects personal autonomy, so that every person is socialized from the time of early childhood to feel he or she has the right to say no, to exert control over his or her own reality and to fulfill his or her own potential. To bring about such change women need to engage in the dominant discourse, which is democracy; we must perceive the question of empowerment as being an issue of citizenship and democracy as well as one of respect for women.

Third, the images of women projected, not only in brochures but also in posters produced by anti-violence groups, are those of women who have been completely devastated: they are beaten, bloodied, sad—broken like dolls, crushed like roses. They are represented as damsels in distress who need to be rescued—yesterday by a knight, today by other women, by institutions or people of good will. Such representations condemn women to perpetual victimization; they will always need somebody to pick them up and put the pieces back together again.

The Institutionalization of Gender Awareness

A similar set of assumptions also pervades much of the diagnosis of problems and training programmes to confront it done by a variety of specialized institutions, governmental and non-governmental.

From the women's movement's "years of protests and proposals" the government heard what was most relevant, just as the movement had demanded. Much of the feminist discourse has now been adopted by government agencies set up to deal with gender violence. Unfortunately, however, these programmes, with a few exceptions, have ignored the sector which has had years of experience in this area; despite its proven effectiveness, the women's movement has been unable to insert itself in these programmes. As a result, training for public servants is directed primarily toward the technical elements of a rigid judicial system, lacking the sensitivity needed for an integrated understanding of the problem.

This situation produces two consequences: first, the persistence of myths and taboos which blame the victim; second, a view of the problem as an individual rather than a social one, a view which explains aggression as a thing which only happens to certain women, without considering the structural dimension of the phenomenon, thereby neutralizing its potential for change. COVAC became aware of this in the course of its own training programmes as well as its work with government agencies conducting training programmes. Looking back over this experience we came to the following conclusions:

The great achievement of feminism in making gender violence a matter of public concern is being eroded by the prevailing form of institutional intervention, in which gender violence is medicalized, measured, professionalized. Intervention tends to be applied in unrelated fragments, according to the training of the professional involved, with no connection to other perspectives. Victims of gender violence are therefore treated within prescribed conceptual frameworks, in which the social subject appears as interacting at the individual level, with other subjects who are similarly isolated. Once victims are placed in an isolated context, outside of other relationships in which they may be engaged, all that can be done is give them therapy. Missing is an integrated perspective or a reflection on the structural condition of women as an element of analysis for recovery.

Training of this kind tends to explain gender violence by reference to the "masochism" or low-life proclivities said to be inherent in many women. Such an explanation assumes every individual to be autonomous, free, capable of choosing among clear and ponderable alternatives. Lacking an understanding of the structural factors which can assail the most rational human life, it explains their behaviour in terms of pathology.

Situations of gender violence are seen as the product of individuals' "personal deficiencies," of maladjustment or disfunction, and solutions are offered that require them to adjust to frequently unjust social structures. This kind of "aidism," though it may help some women, in the long run reinforces their dependence on a third party (for instance, the government) as the means for mitigating their oppression, but not as an instrument to be used for change.

Constructing an Alternative Discourse

Recognizing the limitations of this training model, COVAC has developed a "deconstruction" of the aidist discourse, working throughout the country with groups that are open, mixed, private, NGOs, and with a broad sector of professionals who manage government programmes of service to victims of gender violence.

In order to develop an alternative discourse, COVAC first designed a public opinion poll, conducted by public opinion specialists, designed to discover the views of ordinary people about the degree of violence occurring in the Mexican family, their ideas about the consequences of this violence and the population which is most subject to it.

Conducted in nine states, in areas with local service programmes, publicity, prevention and education about the issue, the poll also collected data about the legal perception of the problem, the effectiveness of the law, the need for new judicial instruments and about the kind of institutions and services needed to deal with violence in the family. A total of 3,600 Mexican households were included, in order to have a solid basis for arguing the need for legislation addressing family violence.

"An Opinion Poll on Violence in the Family" revealed that violence in Mexican households is serious, widespread, and frequent, at least in the urban sector. This was the view of seven out of ten respondents, more than a third of whom said that violence had been a problem in their own family in the last six months. Of the latter, 74 percent reported female victims— 52 percent wives, 30 percent daughters, and 18 percent other female relatives—while 26 percent reported male victims, primarily those between the ages of 5 and 24. Aggressors were believed to be male, most commonly fathers.

The poll also showed that most citizens, both men and women, accurately perceive the devastating effects of this phenomenon, in terms of its physical and mental harm to individuals as well as its broader social impact, including family disintegration, separation and divorce.

Another finding concerned the distance citizens feel from the judicial process. In only 20 percent of cases where abuse had occurred had a complaint been filed; those who did not file explained fear of provoking more violence or fear that the abuser would be jailed. In cases were a complaint was filed, 35 percent were said to have failed. Respondents expressed confusion about which agency to report to as well as a belief that nothing would be done.

In terms of dealing with family violence, while most (74%) respondents felt that those who exercise extreme violence against a family member should be put in jail, 94 percent felt shelters should be more easily available to victims, offering family and individual therapy as well as medical attention, temporary housing, and legal advice.

One of the objectives of the report, in addition to compiling a reliable data base, was to promote further training in these communities, and to expand the dialogue on the issue to include opinion leaders, activists, local legislators, professionals and communications specialists. Thus it concludes by reaffirming the validity of community work, with its broad impact on citizens, and argues that what is needed is improved channels of communication between citizens and the government in order to establish consensual solutions to the problem.

Democracy and Citizenry: Preventing Gender Violence

Armed with the results of the opinion poll, COVAC has begun to construct an alternative discourse, one that grows out of years of experience with abused women and children. The opinion-poll findings confirmed the conclusions drawn from COVAC's experience: given its devastating effects, both at the personal level and at the level of civil society, gender violence should form a substantial part of the both the feminist and the democracy movements. Victims of family violence are excluded from family decisions and the education of their children. Control imposed by violence makes them vulnerable and fearful, and they become unsure of themselves both in their own minds and in relation to others. Many experience a constant paralysis, both as they try to deal with the events of their daily lives and in terms of their own life goals.

Gender violence impedes a woman's having even a minimally desirable quality of life. Women and children who live in violent families may grow, but many of them will never develop into fully autonomous adults, since freedom, a condition essential to human beings, is unknown to them. Democracy, both as a structure for personal life and for one's role as a citizen, remains a utopia for women in a context of violence, attainable only though a rupture in the family order in which they live or through survival mechanisms which are often beyond their reach, given their great social isolation. For children, the family as a place of safety and affection remains a dream. Citizenship, defined as having the minimum conditions necessary in order to exercise one's full rights, is unimaginable for these women: not because they are ignorant or careless, but because the obstacle is created within their own family, perpetuating their condition as "underaged" or "minors" rather than full human beings and citizens.

Oppressed not only because of their gender but also due to the violence, these women are third-class citizens: they participate even less in public life than women who are not abused; they have lower levels of education and are more frequently sick, both physically and psychically. The working days lost due to illness and shame or, at best, in seeking legal remedies to their problems, are translated into high social costs which we have not yet been able to fully evaluate. When added to the demonstrable feminization of poverty throughout Latin America and the Caribbean, the widespread existence of gender violence results in a society of people who are damaged, unproductive, non-participatory.

We maintain that the absence of violence toward women is a necessary ingredient of the new concept of citizenship, in terms of possibilities of choosing and participating. Abused women represent a wasted potential of energy and abilities for any country. Thus reliable data on the phenomenon of gender violence itself constitutes an indicator of the quality of life of a nation.

For all of these reasons, violence against women and children constitutes an obstacle to the development of a country, making it essential to raise awareness among citizens in general, and among abused women in particular, about the need to mobilize at different levels, beginning with direct changes within the family and extending to social and civil organizations. We need to "citizenize" the services offered by government agencies in the broadest sense, allowing these agencies to be influenced and monitored by citizens with an awareness of the need to eradicate gender violence. We need to mount a major campaign to participate in technical advisory bodies, to influence the direction and goals of agencies specializing in sex crimes, centers providing education and assistance in dealing with intra-family violence, hospital services and all agencies which are engage in efforts to democratize public life.

In this sense, the groups which form part of the feminist movement, the broad social sectors of women, and the NGOs working to end gender violence, all have an active role to play as mediators, since they are the bridge between the government and its citizenry; traditionally, these organizations have generated the most well-thought-out and well-substantiated proposals for legislation and public policy. To date, the Mexican government has not considered gender violence as an integral part of the structural condition of women in society, and thus a public issue. Women are still regarded as better off at home, as long as they continue to be productive—in other words, working the traditional "double shift" and not worrying about their rights as citizens, thus: being unfinished citizens. But viewed in the framework of citizenship and democracy, it is clearly essential that government at every level join the effort to turn what until now has been solely women's responsibility into the responsibility of the entire community.

From Victimization to Empowerment

Central to this approach is the recognition that combatting gender violence necessarily involves living with an "attitude of discomfort," working in service and support programmes which offer multiple solutions rather than certainties. Instead of making assumptions about violence and designing therapy for its victims, a series of approaches are needed, approaches which cannot be summed up in pronouncements, mottos or slogans. We must be careful not to accept violence as a natural phenomenon; what is needed is an ongoing search for other ways of understanding which may be latent but which can offer broader and more diverse visions of the phenomenon.

The path which leads from being a victim of violence to having the power to define one's own life, a life with children and a family, in a context of true negotiation with one's partner and the rest of the community, necessarily goes through the issue of subjective experience, in order to get rid of that label. Taking that path is not sufficient to achieve change; it is essential that the victim's environment support and reinforce the power to make the change. It is also important for that environment to include a state which understands that women who are active in their own interests constitute, ethically and politically, a source of citizen strength—they may question the existing vision of women, men and the way they interact, but they will also help to provide a new vision.

It is important that the discourse on the ability to be or to do prevail over the discourse of the victim. The empowerment of women is a concept which implies gaining dignity and thus requires a process which is necessarily individual. This is true for two reasons: the need to develop the ability to plan and to carry out deliberate actions (decision) and the need to improve the degree of autonomy of an individual, which is inseparable from the degree of autonomy of the social group to which the individual belongs (structure).

In societies where violence is harboured as a way of resolving conflicts, societies in which an authoritarian rather than a negotiated solution to differences prevails, we find high indices of violence against women. For this reason, we believe that empowerment will involve work at the individual level, but even more at the community level. While this is true in most countries, in Mexico, as in other countries of the region and throughout the developing world, empowerment also means solving the problems of poverty, malnutrition, housing, health, education and employment, and this represents a task which can only be undertaken by the community, with the help of public polices generated by the government and civil society.

The goal is not to interpret the problem of gender violence but to eliminate it.   ❖

The Power Axis:
Gender Violence in Brazil

HELEIETH I.B. SAFFIOTI

"The phenomena of gender violence, specifically domestic violence, ignores frontiers of any kind: social class, level of industrialization, type of culture, race/ethnic group. It is the most democratic of all social phenomena: it is everywhere, reaching even people above suspicion."

B razilian society is divided along three major lines: race/ethnicity, social class, and gender. These divisions result in distinct hierarchies based on social identities, which while equally important, are not equally active in all historical circumstances; the situation tends to emphasize one or another (Lauretis 1987). As the identities are social rather than psychological, they are actively interwoven in such a way that the resulting knot becomes important. The knot itself must be understood in order to bring about social change. Thus while the hierarchies can be isolated for analysis, the need to recompose the whole demands a focus on the knot. In this conceptual universe, class is no longer sexually or racially undifferentiated, while gender and race do not constitute internal class divisions but categories welded to class.

In terms of class, the income distribution in Brazil is the most unequal in the world. In 1993, the top 5 percent of the resident population received over 40 percent of the national income, with only some 1.7 percent of the economically active population receiving almost one fourth (24%) of the wealth produced in the country. At the other end, over one quarter (26.9%) of the working population received only 6.4 percent of the total national wealth. Blacks and women received the lowest salaries (FIBGE 1993).

Collapsing the three hierarchies, moreover, we see that rich, white men are at the top of the power ladder in Brazil while black, poor women are at the bottom.[1] The intermediate positions—black man and white woman— are interchangeable in economic terms. In 1990, women's income was, on average, 55.7 percent of men's income. White women were in second place, earning 55.3 percent of what white men at the top earned. Black men were third, receiving 48.7 percent of earnings by the top white men. Last were black women, making only 27.6 percent of the white male salaries.[2]

Cutting across the complexities of race and class in Brazil is one phenomenon that permeates all social categories: gender violence, especially domestic violence.

Domestic Violence

Domestic violence is not easy to define. It does not coincide exactly with gender violence, although it occurs within the domestic space. Gender violence is much broader, in that gender prescribes norms not only for men-women relations but also men-men and women-women relations. According to one theory, "Domestic violence has a gender: masculine, whatever the physical sex of the domineering person" (Welzer-Lang 1991:278). This means that the male marks his territory, within which he is sovereign and allowed to punish women and children—even with death. As patriarch, he is in charge of domestication of the people living in that space, although he may delegate part of these functions to women, especially regarding children. As socializers, women fulfill masculine designs at the same time as they tame the young, thereby reaffirming the gender status quo.

Real life, however, requires another type of analysis. Like the rooster, man establishes his territorial dominion: he is absolute master, followed by woman, children and servants, who occupy a position similar to the children. In Brazil, servant girls are often obliged to render sexual favours to the man or to his son. When domestic violence embraces non-related persons it is understood as within the family nucleus. In effect, the two modes of violence overlap; both occur in the midst of affect relationships, with an even more serious issue for domestic violence: daily relationships.

The preferred victims of family violence are women and children. While women administer physical and emotional punishment to children, their slaps are lighter than those of men.[3] Although male authority in itself constitutes such a threat that usually beating is not necessary, when it does occur, it is heavy, often resulting in bone fractures and other serious bodily harm. As for women, they constitute a permanent target for male power and its opposite: male impotence. In fact, impotence is the other side of power. While women, who are socialized to deal with impotence, still find it hard, for men, who are raised for power, the experience is much more difficult. As a result, I believe that violence most often springs from the incapacity to experience impotency, or what I have called a "small-power syndrome" (Saffioti 1989; Saffioti and Almeida 1995). Thus, when power is enjoyed only in one or two dimensions, it is not enough. In terms of class, for example, except for an elite, all are dominated/exploited. While men enjoy power in gender relations, this does not enable them to change the prevailing class power relations. Thus their gender power is a small power, employed to compensate for domination in other areas. The small-power syndrome is, in fact, an experience of impotency.

A large percentage of Brazilian men suffer from this condition. In order to estimate its extent, we have to rely on the only existing study, done in 1988 (FIBGE 1990). This concerns only physical aggression, and does not distinguish between domestic and non-domestic violence, but since most domestic violence takes place in the home and most non-domestic violence takes place in public places, we can construct a reasonably accurate picture from this survey. Among cases of physical aggression in the home, the study found that 63 percent targeted women. Only 37 percent of the victims were men. Among women, 90 percent were from 18 to 49 years old, an age range in which they would normally be married. It would seem reasonable to suppose, therefore, that a large part of these aggressions were caused by their companions. Between 0 and 9 years of age, the proportion of women victims was very low: 3 percent. Between the ages of 10 to 17, this number went up to 8.7 percent, while for women over 50 it was 8.2 percent. In this last group there is a high probability of women being either widowed or separated; between 10 and 17 however, there is quite a large group who, although not in a stable relationship do have active sexual lives with their boyfriends, and consequently, share some time together.

Among men the incidence of physical agression in the home is distributed much more homogeneously across the age spectrum. Under 17 years of age, the proportion of men who are victims is 20.3 percent; increasing to 31 percent among men aged 18 to 19; 33 percent among men aged 30 to 49; and 16 percent among men over 50. Thus among both the youngest and the oldest age cohorts, the percentages are practically twice those of women, which suggests male involvement in violent relations with other men throughout their lives. Although once in a while a man will be hit by a woman, this does not show up statistically, primarily owing to man's greater physical strength and the social incentive men have to act violently. It is likely, therefore, that men suffer violence at the hands of other men; a little over a third of them suffer physical aggression in the home. If there are women who engage in physical struggle with other women, this is much less relevant statistically than women beaten by men. For children, boys or girls, a large part of home violence is committed by parents. At later ages, both sexes may be victims of adults, often their own children.

In public spaces, men are the main targets of physical aggression, making up 87 percent of the victims in commercial buildings, 68 percent of the cases in public streets, 73 percent of cases in schools, and 90 percent of cases in sports stadiums. Relatives predominate as physical aggressors in the home: 52.3 percent. In public areas, unknown aggressors or police together account for 83 percent in commercial buildings and 90.6 percent on public streets. In stadiums, the attackers are the police: 61.3 percent.

Among victims of family violence, two-thirds (66%) of the targets are women. Females aged 0 to 9 are only 2.8 percent of the victims; those from 10 to 17, are 9.9 percent; those from 18 to 29, are 43.6 percent; those aged 30 to 49, 38.4 percent and those 50 and over, 5.3 percent. Once again, the age groups preferred by the aggressors coincide with those in which women are generally married, suggesting that the women are beaten by their companions.

Among male victims of family violence there is again homogeneity across the age spectrum: of such victims ages 1 to 9, 8.1 percent are males; ages 10 to 17, 18.4 percent are male; ages 18 to 29, 30.8 percent are male; ages 30 to 49, 28.4 percent are male and of victims over 50 years old, 14.3 percent are males. Males tend to suffer physical aggression only once, while females are more often subject to repeated violence. When the aggressor is known but unrelated, the proportion of victims is inverted: two thirds are men and only one third are women. In addition, men represent 88 percent of the victims of police violence; all of the victims of violence by private security workers; and 65 percent of victims beaten by unknown aggressors.

While the Legislative Committee of Inquiry collects more specific information on violence against women, the data unfortunately constitute a closed universe; thus we cannot ascertain how much they represent in terms of violence committed against all human beings, women and men. What these data do show are some regional differences. In the south of the country, there are higher numbers of bodily lesions whereas, in the northeast, the percentages of rape and homicide of women by their companions is frightening.

There are no national data on sexual violence in Brazil, although the high incidence of marital rape is well-known. Although the Brazilian Civil Code specifies the performance of "marital duty" for both spouses, it exists, de facto, only for women. This means that when the husband wishes to have sexual relations, the wife fulfills a marital duty by obliging even if it is not what she wishes at that moment. Women agree not only in obedience to the husband but also because "men will go after it outside the house if he can't get it at home," as women frequently testified. If women refuse, however, men can use force. While outside marriage, rape is a crime subject to 6 to 10 years imprisonment, marital rape is not included in the Penal Code. While it is considered an incidence of domestic and family violence, and thus subject to investigation by police, it is usually very hard to prove.

Regarding sexual violence against children, the incidence is much higher than generally imagined. Although also committed by strangers, the great majority of sexual-abuse cases against children occur within the family. In a study of incest abuse within 50 families in São Paulo, findings were similar to those in other countries. Contrary to what was thought, adolescence, the time of life when the secondary sexual characteristics bloom and girls become exuberant, is not the preferred age of aggressors. Sexual aggression may begin with babies and continue throughout adolescence, but it usually starts between 7 and 10 years of age. Within the 50 families, all of whom had reported abuse, there were 52 aggressors, all of whom were men, and 63 victims, all of whom were girls. Of the aggressors, 37 were biological fathers and 6 were stepfathers; 11 of the girls gave birth to their fathers' children. Other relatives who inflicted violence against children included cousin, uncle, grandfather, brother-in-law (Saffioti 1993, 1995, 1997).

Although children of both sexes are subject to child sexual abuse, international statistics show that 90 percent of the victims of this type of violence are girls as opposed to 10 percent boys. The aggressors are, almost always, men. It is estimated that between 1 and 3 percent of sexual aggressors are women (Clarac and Bonnin 1985; Rush 1980). The abuse takes various forms. Boys are usually victims of anal penetration, although not exclusively. Oral sex is also frequently performed by both boys and girls on adult men. Girls are the favorite target of domestic sexual aggressors.

Like physical violence, sexual abuse occurs in all social classes, differing only in the approaches. In the popular strata, the use or threat of physical violence to commit sexual abuse is more frequent. In the richer and better educated strata, the most frequent approach is seduction. It is difficult to say which approach causes more harm. In-depth interviews with the 63 victims indicated more serious damage through seduction. When the child is brutally raped, with a threat of death and a visible knife, it is inevitable. The child is paralyzed by fear; there is no possible resistance. Inter-family sexual abuse through seduction involves a child emotionally, making him or her a co-participant, at least, in terms of self-perception. Typically, the child does not see itself as victim, but instead feels enormous guilt.[4]

Domestic violence, especially sexual abuse, has always been a well-kept family secret. It was the feminists who raised the veil of secrecy which still hides many aspects of this phenomenon. Feminists are the overwhelming majority of those studying domestic violence worldwide. In Brazil, there were feminist demonstrations each time a woman was killed by her companion. Not until 1985, however, did the pressure become organized, aimed at making this type of violence visible, stopping it, and punishing its perpetrators.

"Safe Spaces" for Women

During the 1982 campaign for governor of the state of São Paulo, feminist members of the opposition party took up the gender issue and negotiated some agreements, with the result that when the party won, it created the State Council on the Feminine Condition (CECF) in April 1983, less than one month after the governor took office. Other states followed, as did counties and municipalities, and in 1984, the National Council for Women's Rights (CNDM) was created. CNDM played a very important role in the National Constitutional Assembly in 1987-88, which resulted in the draft Federal Constitution of October 1988.

With the co-operation of many feminists, the CECF began with four priority issues: work, education, health and violence. In order to avoid difficult situations for women victims of violence, a policy of creating women-only spaces was devised. One such space was to be specialized police stations to care for women—Defense of Women Police Stations or DDMs, fully run by professional women. A major obstacle to women's filing complaints at police stations—the sexualized approach of police officers at all levels—would be thus eliminated. In effect, the DDMs work in most cases with only female police officers.

In 1985, the first DDM was created in the municipality of São Paulo, followed by several other state and municipal capitals. Today there are 16 DDMs in São Paulo and 109 in interior municipalities. In Brazil as a whole there are approximately 200 of these police stations. Some are well run, others, not so well. There is a lot of variation in the way victims are treated by police officers and there are still DDMs hiring male drivers and detectives.

The original idea, carried out early on, was to educate the police force in gender relations. CECF held several seminars with female police officers and even male sheriffs. Various types of violence were discussed, mainly the domestic type, in the context of gender relations and several existing theories on the theme. Female police officers were prepared to render a high-quality service to women victims of violence. When the government changed four years later, however, the relationship of CECF with the police officers was discontinued. In fact, fragmentation and lack of continuity has characterized all public policy regarding gender violence. Shelters are a case in point: in all of Brazil, a country of 160 million people, there are only four shelters for women. There used to be six shelters, but the demand for resources is very high, thus two were abandoned when they were no longer a priority of the government.

For the most part, experiences with shelters, originally known as SOS Mulher (SOS Woman), were not successful. Resources of all kinds were lacking, along with skills in dealing with women in shelters and the conflicts among them. One successful experience is the Casa de Apoio Viva Maria (Support House Hurrah/Live Maria) in Porto Alegre, in the south of the country. Its management team is highly competent and took care to elaborate a project that anticipates financial resources in the municipal budget, and establishes links between shelter policy and health and housing policies. In Porto Alegre county, 20 percent of public housing units are reserved for women who have been at the Casa, thereby securing the needed resources and integrating the two policies. In addition, the Casa assists women in job searches, enabling them to support themselves apart from the aggressor, and raising women's self-esteem. There are also activities for the children, both at the shelter and in the community.

Another CECF support entity, albeit short-lived, was the Orientation and Support Centre for Women (COJE), created in July 1984. Linked to the São Paulo Justice Secretariat and the state Attorney General's Office, COJE, under the direction of CECF, provided legal and psychological support to women who needed it. In its first six months, COJE registered

20.7 percent victims of domestic violence among its clients, which rose to 29.4 percent in January and 36 percent in February 1995. While providing legal and psychological advice, COJE did a superb job of raising women's consciousness of their rights and the ways to assure these. Unfortunately, during the last six months of 1996 COJE had a new director, who opposed feminist policies, and CECF lost control over this entity.

There were other losses resulting from the indiscriminate establishment of DDMs around the country, particularly in the State of São Paulo. The state paid no attention to the qualification of police officers in terms of gender relations, and failed to provide basic infrastructure such as offices, vehicles, or fuel—thereby spending little but gaining much in terms of political dividends from setting up DDMs.

This may change with the creation of Special Criminal Courts, which were designed to introduce a level of informality and speedy processing of claims. The goal is to bring about, as much as possible, reparation to the victim and sentences designed to correct the behaviour of the offenders rather than restrict their liberty." Since the Special Criminal Courts can deal only with those crimes for which the law does not prescribe a maximum sentence of over one year, they will be in charge of "penal infractions of minor offensive potential."

Although Special Criminal Courts have yet to be set up, the provisions included in their enabling legislation are considered to be in effect, and judges are applying the law as far as possible. For crimes that carry penalities of less than a year, for example, the courts may "suspend the process, submitting the accused to a probation period" during which the accused must obey certain conditions, including: 1) reparation of damage; 2) ban on going to certain places; 3) ban on leaving the municipality of residence without court authorization; 4) mandatory visits to the court, once a month, to inform and justify activities.

There are several advantages of the more informal mediation approach envisioned for these courts. Given the harsh sentences for violence, few offenders are actually convicted (a Globo TV study reveals that only 2 percent of people who attack women go to jail), and those who are convicted have little incentive to change their behaviour, especially in view of the current tendency to impose reclusive sentences rather than educational ones. The conciliation principle may also provide some benefit to women tied to violent men. Many times the woman won't accuse the man because he is the sole family provider, for example. The new courts allow for the re-socialization of the aggressors, thus benefiting women and men alike, as individuals and in their relationships.

The law pertaining to Special Criminal Courts also transforms the penalty for infliction of bodily lesions, frequent in domestic violence, from unconditional to conditional action, meaning that when a complaint is filed, both victim and accused are summoned before a judge, along with their lawyers, to attempt to reach a conciliation. Agreement implies the accused will not appeal and the victim will not sue. When agreement is not possible, and a victim decides to sue, the Public Prosecutor will propose the immediate application of a rights-restrictive sentence or fine, which also carries conditions. In accepting the proposal, the accused avoids a conviction and thus keeps a clean record, while the victim, especially the woman, does not lose the provider of her family. There is, therefore, no apparent damage to the victims. On the contrary, when discussing reparations, as well as penalties or fines, there is an important educational aspect which benefits both victims and aggressors, particularly when the issue is marital violence.

The legislation providing for Special Criminal Courts provoked the DDMs to demand more legal authority. Within the civil police, DDMs are disparagingly referred to as the "police kitchen" because they deal with "tiny issues" concerning family and thus are seen as less important than other police sectors. A recent statewide decree in São Paolo increased the DDM legal authority to deal with crimes against life, specifically homicide, abortion, infanticide, and induced suicide, thereby conferring a degree of *status* that was previously lacking. To date, however, the DDMs have not had a single case of homicide, and some station heads do not consider their units adequately trained to operate in this area. Nevertheless, the new legislation is potentially important, both for the police and for the legal treatment of violence, specially domestic, which has as main targets women, children and teenagers.

Conclusions

There is a widespread belief that economic development eliminates, or at least reduces, discrimination against women. Once in the marketplace, the argument goes, women can potentially attain a status very close to that of men. This assumption, however, is a fallacy. The phenomena of gender violence, specifically domestic violence, ignores frontiers of any kind: social class, level of industrialization, type of culture, race/ethnic group. It is the most democratic of all social phenomena: it is everywhere, reaching even people above suspicion. Without systematic state intervention, therefore, domestic violence will not be significantly reduced. The state, however, is still highly male-oriented and thus tends to cripple public policies addressed to women (MacKinnon 1989; Saffioti and Almeida 1993), largely through failure to implement them. Thus it is not enough for feminists to formulate these policies; they must create mechanisms to ensure that feminist public-policy specialists participate in their implementation. In this connection, there are a number of ways in which the international community, including UNIFEM, can support efforts of non-governmental organizations (NGOs) to assist the state in implementing policy to reduce domestic violence.

While the DDMs are doubtless a big step forward and must be preserved, their action is very uneven, as each head follows, in the absence of training, her intuition. Public policy of this importance cannot be dependent on the good sense of police officers. NGOs can assist here through training of professional and administrative personnel in gender relations. Like the one-week course that the Council of Women's Rights (CEDIM) did in Rio de Janeiro for graduates of the Police Academy in 1988, or the 28-hour course for commanders and sub-commanders of the Military Police in 1994, there will soon be a course in gender relations for all heads of DDMs of the State of São Paulo. The demand for the course came from the DDM heads themselves, who had participated in a ten-year celebration of the first DDM course on gender relations, in August 1995.

Necessary to good policy are good statistics, especially in a country like Brazil. Until the state can adequately carry out this function, the international community should support collection and classification of data which will permit a view of several aspects related to gender in the country. In addition, there is almost no scientific literature on gender for teenagers. Support to NGOs for the development of educational and pre-school books will be of great value.

While specific projects on shelters for women victims of violence and their children should be supported through the NGO community, their maintenance should be secured by the state through appropriate legislation. A similar partnership should be considered for projects designed to re-educate violent men. In this case, the state should see to the recruitment of the subjects and UNIFEM could pay the professionals who work in the project. Experiences from abroad, especially in Canada, may be adapted to

Brazil. A number of NGOs are prepared to render enormous co-operation in the formulation or implementation of the measures to restrict violence.

Minimum-income programmes should pay special attention to women-headed households, which comprise more than 20 percent of all households. Unlike households headed by men, which usually have two parents, those headed by women, in 98 percent of the cases, only have one parent, in many cases as a result of domestic violence. When there are children under 14, the minimum age to work, conditions are miserable, since women usually make much less than men and the children cannot yet contribute to the family budget. Although these programmes should be undertaken by the state, UNIFEM could support projects aimed at improving the income levels of these families.

Small enterprises, such as electric appliance repair shops, which men no longer operate, could be set up by women with proper training; the tools needed are little more than a screw-driver and pliers. A van would be required to pick up the appliances and distribute the smaller ones among women with small children who could repair them at home. The larger ones would be taken to the shop for repair by women free to leave home. Enterprises of this kind could introduce women to traditionally masculine activities, with prestige and higher profits. Such projects would help to reduce inequalities and make certain roles playable by both women and men, indistinctly. Two fronts would be thus attacked: reduction of female poverty and extreme specialization in professional gender roles.

In the same way that some minimum-income programmes are linked to school attendance on part of children, projects could be developed for women conditioned to non-violence on part of men. Such projects would reflect the spirit of the law which created the special courts, in search of new ways to re-socialize women and men towards a more harmonious companionship.

Social change does not happen quickly or automatically. Rather, state-led affirmative action is necessary to enable women to make up for lost time and gain social equality with men. For this to happen, public policies must be put in place that are grounded in the principle of equity.   ❖

Notes

1. Racism is primarily against blacks, although other ethnic expressions of racism exist. Even blacks can undergo a "whitening" process, if they manage to rise economically or socially. Pélé, the great soccer player and currently Minister of Sports, has married twice, both times to blonde women. However, as blacks are historically associated with poverty, low levels of education and low-paid occupations, individuals who manage to become "white" are very rare.

2. In rural areas, women make 42.1% of what men make, an even wider gap that in the cities. Moreover, while black men earned 56% of white male earnings. White women earned only 36% and black women only 28%.

3. Based on research from Defense of Women Police Stations and at the SOS Child in São Paulo (Saffioti 1996).

4. This type of family abuse is not the same as incest, a phenomenon which takes place between people of the same approximate age, who have a peer relationship, rather than one permeated by power. In incest, there is no violence, as there is in the case of incestuous abuse, there is a large age gap and the link is one of authority.

References

Clarac, V. and N. Bonnin (1985). *De la Honte à la colère*. Poitiers: Les Publications Anonymes.

Fundação Instituto Brasileiro de Geografia e Estatística (FIBGE) (1993). *National Household Survey*. Rio de Janeiro: FIBGE.

_____(1990). *Participacão Político-Social 1988 - Justica e Vitimização*. Rio de Janeiro: FIBGE.

Lauretis, Teresa de (1987). "Preface" and "The Technology of Gender." *In Technologies of Gender*. Bloomington, IN: Indiana University Press.

MacKinnon. K. (1989). *Toward a Feminist Theory of the State*. Cambridge, MA: Harvard University Press.

Rush, F. (1980). *The Best Kept Secret: Sexual Abuse of Children*. New York: McGraw-Hill.

Saffioti, H. (1997). "No Fio da Navalha: Violencia contra Criancas e Adolescentes no Brasil Atual." *In Quem Mandou Nascer Mulher!* Rio de Janeiro: UNICEF/Editora Rosa dos Tempos.

_____ (1995). "Abuso Sexual Pai-Filha." In F. Quintas, ed., *Mulher Negra: preconceito, sexualidade, imaginario*. Recife: Fundação Joaquim Nabuco/Editora Massangana.

_____ (1993). "Circuito Cerrado: Abuso Sexual Incestuoso." *In Vigiladas Y Castigadas*. Lima: CLADEM.

_____ (1989). "A síndrome do pequeno poder." In M.A. Azevedo and V. N. Guerra, eds., *Crianças Vitimizadas: a Síndrome do Pequeno Poder*. São Paulo: Iglu Editora.

Saffioti, H. and S.S. de Almeida (1995). *Violencia de Genero: Poder e Impotencia*. Rio de Janeiro: Zahar Editores.

_____ (1993). "Epistemologia, Estado y Políticas Públicas Dirigidas a la Mujer," *Travesias* 1, Buenos Aires.

Welzer-Lang, D. (1991). *Les Hommes Violents*. Paris: Lierre & Coudrier Editeur.

Beyond the Conventions:
Violence Prevention in the Andean Region

ALEXANDRA AYALA MARÍN

*"The experience of work to prevent violence against women has
demonstrated that one of the most difficult tasks is to penetrate the deeply
engrained cultural norms and assumptions that still make men and male
values the referent for humankind's thinking and behaviour."*

D uring its first year (1994-95), Ecuador's Women and Family Court
received a total of 6,101 complaints concerning violence. Of these, 96
percent were by women, 86 percent of whom had been attacked by
their partners or former partners. In Peru, out of 9,000 complaints to the
Women's Court of Lima in 1993, 95 percent featured husbands or a
woman's male partner.[1] In Colombia, the Women's House in Bogotá
reports that 62 percent of the women requesting advisory assistance
between 1989 and 1991 had problems with violence in their families.
These figures are approximately the same in Venezuela and Bolivia,
according to national reports prepared by NGOs for the 1995 Fourth
World Conference on Women in Beijing. They not only make visible but
also document a reality that until recently has been concealed.

Although official statistics are rarely available, given the reluctance of
relevant governmental agencies to pay attention to this subject, work by
women's non-governmental organizations (NGOs) has documented the
magnitude of gender violence and the implications for its victims. Within
the Andean subregion, the phenomenon of violence is similar in all
countries, whether or not social violence is on the increase, as demonstrated
by data from legal and psychological assistance services. Common to all is
the fact that "the risk factor is being a woman." Regardless of the socio-
economic status, ethnic group, religion, age, urban/rural setting, most
women are subject to violence in various forms, in different social contexts.

However, the most frequent, jolting forms—especially in terms of their
psychological and mental-health consequences—occur within the home:

87

abuse in the couple's relations and sexual violence against girls and young women by fathers, uncles, brothers and/or other relatives. These expressions of violence are also the hardest to denounce, riddled as they are with cultural and emotional factors that hinder attempts to intervene.

Given this common denominator, women's organizations in all of the Andean countries have struggled for over ten years to get laws passed or revised in order to permit intervention in the home, which is where, under the veil of privacy, the greatest number of crimes occur, and typically go unpunished. They have called for the creation of Women's Courts which not only expose the problem but provide a place where victims can have a hearing without being themselves condemned. These are non-police entities created by an agreement between the Ministry of the Interior and women's NGOs, which provide the technical staff (psychologist, attorney and/or social workers). The response has been overwhelming:

"We have four people receiving the complaints, and an amazing demand of 50 cases a day. Sometimes women have to wait, or staff are unwilling to see them. Most of the time, I have to take the charges by hand to speed things up, because we can't make women wait so long to be served," said Victoria Neacato, head of the Women and Family Court of Quito, in a 1996 interview. Her remarks describe the situation women typically face when they bring a complaint—even at such a specialized agency, and reflect the relatively minor importance the government gives to this problem. As a result of poor resources, little political support, and a predominantly male staff which is only minimally trained, the courts do not yet provide the support these women need, or the conviction that aggressors must be punished.

Thus creating and/or strengthening Women's Courts; sensitizing and training justice administration agents and staff as well as all those responsible for citizens' security to protect the rights of women and girls who are victims and/or at risk of violence—are part of the recommendations for national governments. The recommendation for the women's movement is to promote research into the violence in women's lives in order to obtain records that will make it possible to disseminate information, propose, coordinate and implement policies.

Gender violence is a social problem that demands social intervention. According to the Beijing Platform for Action (paragraph 112): "Violence against women makes it impossible to attain the goals of equality, development and peace...it violates, narrows or prevents women's enjoyment of human rights and fundamental freedoms ...." These statements summarize the findings of studies in numerous countries: violence against women is an obstacle to personal and community development, and constitutes a violation of human rights. As long as there is violence against women, failure to respect their human rights, and ignorance of the reasons for their history of subordination and discrimination, it will not be possible to promote their empowerment. For this reason, UNIFEM's Andean office concluded that training in gender and human rights is a strategic way to further the goals of preventing and eradicating violence, strengthening the enjoyment of citizenship, and promoting empowerment.

Since 1994, UNIFEM has provided financial and technical support for a variety of projects, all linked to gender and human-rights training. In Peru, 281 people from the National Police, Justices of the Peace and Women's Courts were trained to process complaints from women who have been victims of aggression. All judges and prosecuting attorneys in Cochabamba, Bolivia, have received gender training. The Gender Training Manual for justice administration personnel—an outgrowth of training female attorneys from Venezuela, Colombia, Ecuador, Peru and Bolivia, and of the replication by these attorneys in their own countries— has broad prospects through the multiplier effects of such actions. These efforts have enabled UNIFEM to lay the groundwork to pursue their main aim: promoting women's empowerment.

Current projects are part of the regional programme to prevent violence against women, which the Andean office announced in December 1994 at a seminar entitled "The Police Institution and Women's Human Rights." [2] This seminar was the culmination of a series of workshops to train female attorneys and judges, held in coordination with the Latin American Human Rights Association (ALDHU), the Centre for Women's Promotion and Action (CEPAM) and the National Bureau of Women (DINAMU).

Since then, UNIFEM has conducted a series of workshops and seminars in the various countries of the subregion, offering training in gender and women's human rights, targeting male and female legal professionals and academics, judges, specialized court judges, police staff, radio communicators, and indigenous and peasant audiences. These activities have been oriented towards making violence against women visible; sensitizing the citizenry, states and justice personnel, raising their consciousness and, above all consolidating that gender awareness that is so necessary in order to effectively undertake other relationships that can ensure respect for women's human rights.

The reason for targeting legal and justice administration personnel is the belief that preventing violence requires not only legal reform but the creation of new attitudes and worldviews as well as the political will to ensure that law enforcement will be guided by an accurate understanding of legal equality for men and women. The goal is to discover the male-centredness that pervades both the spirit of the law and the mentality of men and women. As Alda Facio points out, "in most cases, different outlooks on reality are male-centred, and have therefore failed to take women's experiences and viewpoints into account; this has cloaked the daily violations of their human rights in invisibility, along with a slighting of their needs as human beings and consequently construed legal equality with a male referent. [3] In order to understand violence against women as one of the manifold expressions of imbalanced power relations between men and women it is necessary to de-mystify the roots of this male-centred thought that permeates societies.

Prevention for Empowerment

Understanding empowerment as "appropriation, interiorization and wielding of power" entails a concept of citizenship that involves "knowing what women's rights and duties are in society." [4] This concept grows out of the creation and/or consolidation of gender awareness with the capacity to counteract the obstacles that stand in the way of enjoyment of citizenship. These obstacles include people's lack of awareness of their human rights, and the violence that they are subject to, in both public and private situations. If the goal is to promote women's empowerment, it is necessary to clear away such obstacles.

Beginning in the late 1970s, actions to address violence were initiated by NGOs in all countries of the subregion, especially through legal advisory support for abused women.[5] By the end of the 1980s, all five countries (Bolivia, Colombia, Ecuador, Peru, Venezuela) had NGOs providing at least some legal and/or psychological care, and specialized services to help battered women. Studies in each country began to reveal the problem's magnitude.[6] More recently, NGOs have begun to form coalitions such as the Latin American and Caribbean Network Against Sexual and Domestic Violence, which works for full enforcement of women's human rights through prevention, punishment and elimination of violence.

After ten years of intense activities by organized women, one might expect that violence against women would be significantly reduced. All five countries have signed the 1981 Convention for the Elimination of All Forms of Discrimination Against Women (CEDAW), the Declaration and Action Programme from Vienna (1993), and the Beijing Declaration and Platform for Action (1995). All but Colombia have ratified the 1994 Inter-American Convention to Prevent, Sanction and Eradicate Violence Against Women (Belem Convention), and signed the 1993 UN Declaration on the Elimination of Violence Against Women.

Laws and policies have also undergone review and change. In Venezuela, the National Women's Council drafted a Law Against Domestic and Sexual Violence in 1993; in Ecuador the National Women's Bureau lobbied female attorneys and NGOs to formulate the Law Against Violence Affecting Women and Families, passed in November 1995; in Bolivia, the Under-Secretariat of Gender Issues formulated the National Plan to Prevent and Eradicate Violence Against Women, enacting the corresponding law in 1996. In addition, government agencies at various levels now deal with women's policies and projects, and have pushed for laws against violence. At the parliamentary level, there are commissions to legislate on topics related to women and families. Peru, Ecuador and Bolivia now have Women's Courts, and Colombia has Family Courts, which have begun to work together with women's NGOs.

In addition, gender-related violence has become an issue for discussion in universities, through conferences, seminars and lectures in the different countries, through the Women's Studies Centre of the Central University of Venezuela, founded in 1992. In Bolivia, the National Plan to Prevent and Eradicate Violence against Women provides for inclusion in primary and secondary schools' curricular and extracurricular activities of subjects that can help create an awareness of this problem.

Despite these achievements, however, it remains true that governments generally do not display enough political will to implement mechanisms that would genuinely help to prevent this problem. Justice administration personnel know little about international conventions that their governments have signed, and they often rule in flagrant contradiction to the provisions of the CEDAW, or the Vienna Declaration. Moreover, relevant bodies do little to collect or disseminate information about gender violence. Women's Courts are poorly funded, short staffed and insufficiently trained. Specific laws are not always enforced; those administering justice are unaware of them, or interpret them according to male-centred criteria. Enforcement is restricted by lack of financial resources, such as in Peru, where a law on intra-family violence has been on the books since 1992, and in Ecuador, where the law was passed in November 1995, but corresponding regulations are still pending.

Finally, despite international commitments and ad hoc laws, other bodies of law, such as criminal law and procedure codes, not only feature discriminatory standards which "uphold women's role as fundamentally involving sexuality and motherhood," but treat women the same as handicapped or elderly persons. [7] As Alda Facio notes: "Law remains patriarchal, although over the centuries the anti-woman legislation has developed greater subtlety."[8]

To deal with this legal discrimination, NGOs of all five countries have presented proposals for reforms geared to make a place in the law for women, as complete human beings, and not only in their reproductive facets; to abandon the use of value-laden terminology (such as "forcing of a virtuous woman" to mean rape); and to establish that a sexual crime violates a person's right to self-determination.

Participatory Methodology and Multiplier Effects

Responding to the demands of the women's movement, UNIFEM supports a number of projects designed to address these problems. A Data Bank on violence in Ecuador and analysis of legislation on violence in Latin America and the Caribbean both aim to cover information gaps so that longer-term actions can be planned. Similarly, in an effort to change deep-seated cultural attitudes, not only justice administration personnel but also communicators and radio staff are being trained in gender violence, in Bolivia, Peru and Ecuador.

In a year and a half, the Campaign for Communication Against Domestic Violence in Bolivia has tripled news coverage of this subject; denouncements in existing services have increased; there is ongoing demand for greater information and opinion leaders refer to the problem in their public speeches. The Under-Secretariat of Gender Affairs (SAG), under the Ministry of Human Development, establishes systematic contacts with local radio stations throughout the country, and 60 national stations broadcast data-based messages rather than rhetoric or propaganda. Broadcasts include information about legal reforms and existing services, the status of Bolivian women, the nature of domestic violence and the new patterns of social behaviour needed to address this problem. Information has also been distributed to provincial newspapers throughout the country, especially in rural areas, and workshops have been held to sensitize and train male and female social communicators.

Notwithstanding these encouraging results, there are a number of limitations. One is the lack of resources to permit systematic follow-up to measure impact. This will affect the quality of messages, which require ongoing feedback as well as local production so the audience can identify with them. SAG evaluators recommend budgeting not only for impact assessment and follow-up mechanisms, but especially thinking about production teams to make newscasts and/or programmes with local situations and actors.

Through the project on Promotion of Peasant and Indigenous Women's Rights, training in gender, women's human rights and violence has been provided for radio station staff in rural areas of Peru and Ecuador. One of the trainees stated: "Since the workshop, I have been trying to apply, in my work, what I learned. I attempt to conduct interviews and provide information with a gender perspective. I belong to a neighborhood radio station, and we have begun a programme with the gender approach, in which we began by addressing violence against women, because it is a very frequent problem in that barrio." [9]

Filling Information Gaps

Under the leadership of the María Guare Foundation, an NGO specializing in violence prevention, systematic data on violence against women in now being gathered for the first time. Regular bulletins publicize court decisions along with information about various aspects of violence, based on the charges made in the court. The information has substantiated two claims: that domestic violence is a social problem, and that most victims are women. Not only were 96 percent of those presenting complaints women, 82 percent of cases of aggression happened within the home, and victims have been of all ages (with the greatest number of cases between 16 and 35 years).

Each time a bulletin comes out, the media broadcast its data, keeping their audiences up to date with accurate figures about a problem that people have talked about, but had not adequately denounced. Anunziatta Valdez, María Guare Foundation president, explains: "making violence visible is the data bank's fundamental strategy, making domestic and sexual violence against women, girls and boys known so that it will no longer be permissible".

Data recorded on report sheets reflect socio-economic and cultural aspects of the person presenting the claim, the type and place of aggression, relationship between the victim and aggressor, including reactions to the violent action, and consequences in the family's life. These data, systematized by the computer software, are ordered as graphs and charts for publication. Most importantly, the data permit a detailed reading, cross-referencing variables to analyze the problem, with an eye to broader policies to prevent violence against women.

After two years, the Data Bank has become an indispensable complement to the Court, and the only way that the citizenry can learn of the magnitude of this social problem and think about measures to eradicate it. Its information can help both government and international agencies design policies to improve the situation of women and children. It has influenced the other four Women and Family Courts in Ecuador to include statistical information as an essential element of their operations, and the government to plan to set up a nation-wide data bank.

However, the real obstacles to reducing violence against women are the lack of importance the state gives the Women and Family Courts, much less to systematizing data on violence against women. Official statistics ignore these realities, because official agencies care little about preventing violence against women, as reflected in the lack of budget allocations.

Training: Targeting Strategic Players

The project for Advisory Support and Training in Receiving Denouncements regarding Family Violence, implemented by the Flora Tristan Centre in Peru, spread to ten of Peru's largest cities and four municipalities of Metropolitan Lima. Targeting strategic players in the police and the justice system, training workshops on women's human rights have been held in the context of addressing intra-family and sexual violence. These have reached a wide range of people, including police officers and staff, NGO members, grassroots organization leaders and members, physicians working in legal applications, provincial prosecutors, female legal promoters, journalists, state functionaries, councilwomen and students.

In comparing the responses to a questionnaire passed out at the beginning of the workshop with a test on resolving a case of family or sexual violence given at the end, evaluators found progress in handling the new concepts on how to treat battered women, expressed in more humane, solidary care provision. Impact can also be measured by the broad assortment of audiences, in different parts of the country. The Flora Tristán Centre was also invited to take part in preparing the National Human Rights Report (the first such invitation for a women's organization), and to include women's vision. And as a result of sensitizing the executive secretary of the Human Rights Commission, there is the possibility of holding joint activities with the Women's Court officers nationwide.

Research and Analysis of Laws

An international study of 14 countries regarding the contents and forms of legislation about violence against women was coordinated in the Andean region by the Gender and Power Programme of the Latin American Institute of Alternative Legal Services (ILSA), headquartered in Bogotá. The study compared legislative trends in Latin America and the Caribbean, analyzed law enforcement by the police, government agencies and judicial system, and examined institutional and cultural difficulties in confronting domestic violence. Its findings were grounded in a broad-based survey of women's and human-rights groups, action networks and feminists who address this problem on a day-to-day basis.

The study found that Latin America, contrary to what has been claimed, stands out for the systematization of its gender-violence training, especially for police and justice-system personnel. It recommended that NGOs place the issue of domestic violence against women on the overall political agenda, within the human-rights context, in order to interest executive, legislative and judicial entities. It noted that broad, nationwide campaigns must be organized to disseminate information beyond the capital cities.

In addition to informing the UN Special Report on Violence Against Women in 1995, the study encouraged discussion of the issue throughout the region. Early findings were presented at the Fourth World Conference on Women in Beijing in 1995. The response indicated growing demand for government responsibility to reform relevant legislation.

Gender Training with a Long-Term Outlook

The Gender Training Manual for justice administration system personnel of the Andean countries, supported by UNIFEM, is notable for its methodology based on practical training to provide feedback. The Manual's contents embrace the heterogeneity and common points of these five countries, to reinterpret the law with a gender approach in order to inform and sensitize about women's human rights, gender violence and its consequences. It addresses the common fact that the target audience is not exactly eager to change, being accustomed to seeing reality and the law through male-centred concepts.

The practical training process which produced the Manual began in May 1995, when female attorneys and judges, representing government and non-government agencies, academic institutions, and indigenous groups, met in Quito to prepare the preliminary version of the Training Manual, using a participatory methodology. The participants' commitment to replicate the workshop in their own countries was sought in order to adjust training to their own realities.

In July 1996, a second workshop enabled participants to discuss the final draft on the basis of experience in workshops held in their own countries. Training workshops have been replicated in Bolivia, Ecuador and Peru, coordinated with government and/or non-governmental agencies, bar associations and judicial bodies, such as the Supreme Court of Justice in Ecuador.[10] Workshops in each country were extraordinarily well attended: in Cochabamba, Bolivia, for example, every judge in town participated. Special efforts were also made to include Indian judges. In Peru, as a result, judges working with the Aguaruna and Shipibo-Conibo peoples of the Amazon region attended.

One of the most significant achievements of training in each country was breaking down the resistance of most participants, especially the men, who are unaccustomed to looking at legal postulates and traditional thinking about women in a new way. Justice personnel have generally been trained with the conviction that the spirit of the law is immovable, in addition to the unconscious male-centred approach that makes men and maleness the centre of human thinking and the law. This is manifested, for example, in ignoring international conventions and declarations regarding women's rights that States have signed. As Claudia Cáceres, former Ministry of Justice staff member from Colombia, states: "Women feel that they, as judges or magistrates, are not affected by discrimination, and men feel attacked." Yet when participants become receptive, the training will be much more successful. An important recommendation in this regard, made by male attendees, is that some trainers be men. It is also worth noting that the president of the Association of Magistrates of Cochabamba, for example, admitted (in the closing ceremony) that he had been mistaken in expecting the workshop to be a waste of time.

Reflections

Intervention by UNIFEM's Andean office in prevention of violence against women is grounded in the needs and proposals of the women's movement in the subregion. As such, it has major repercussions. Each of the projects produces complementary chain reactions, laying the groundwork for the single overall aim of women's empowerment. Empowerment is a goal that will remain unreachable as long as women's human rights are ignored, and as long as violence is a reality that is concealed: the more it is hidden away, the stronger will remain the obstacles preventing women from enjoying the rights that they need to build their citizenship.

Because training is participatory, it begins by sensitizing, attempting to break through existing attitudes with other knowledge and other ways of reading realities, which is the gender approach. For this reason, groups are targeted because of their ability, on the basis of their diversity and location, to become multipliers—not only to convey knowledge through new training events, but especially in the way they treat women violence victims and the way they understand the problem. Police men and women, judges, attorneys, prosecutors, journalists, and the entire project beneficiary population have been well enough trained in UNIFEM's projects to guarantee this multiplier effect, not only in the main cities, but also in smaller towns, generally far away from more influential urban centres, and reach the rural sectors through radio broadcasts.

One conclusion is evident: preventing violence against women requires the many-faceted efforts and coordination of various sectors to maximize resources and make actions more effective. Despite women's NGOs' intensive struggle, despite the enactment of special laws or creation of Women's Courts, despite support from UNIFEM and other UN agencies— much remains to be done. Above all, states must demonstrate the political will to address the problem more effectively, in order to comply with the international conventions related to women's rights and prevention of gender-related violence.

Government allocation of economic resources is indispensable to the prevention of violence. Most of the work is done by NGOs, all of which require funds to undertake specific sensitization and training activities. All are experiencing increasing difficulty in obtaining international funding, especially when the target population is the professional sector; "funding agencies fail to see the multiplier effect that this type of work can have," according to Julieta Montaño, a Bolivian attorney.

The experience of work to prevent violence against women has demonstrated that one of the most difficult tasks is to penetrate the deeply engrained cultural norms and assumptions that still make men and male values the referent for humankind's thinking and behaviour. This is most visible, as already pointed out, among people such as justice administration personnel, generally accustomed to interpreting reality through the eyes of the law and its male-centred contents. However, as María Helena Reyes, a Peruvian attorney who participated in the workshops, put it, "It is no easy matter to train justice-administration personnel in gender. In formal law, it is necessary to break through many symbols in order to break down traditional behaviour patterns regarding women. However, this training is a challenge, and a job that must be done."   ❖

Notes

1. Luis E. Delgado Villena, "Conocer los derechos de la vida en pareja," in *La institución policial y los derechos humanos de las mujeres* (Quito: UNIFEM, 1995), p. 122.

2. Representatives of the police, government and NGOs from nine South American countries shared experience of courts specialized in serving victims of violence. See Alexandra Ayala Marin, "Women's Human Rights and the Police: An Andean Regional Seminar," in Ana Maria Brasileiro, ed., *Building Democracy with Women* (New York: UNIFEM, 1996).

3. See Aldo Facio, "The Principle of Equality Before the Law," in *Women's Human Rights: Conceptual Approaches* (Lima: UNIFEM, 1996), pp. 82-83.

4. Mónica Muñoz-Vargas, "Hacia el empoderamiento y la ciudadanía de las mujeres," *Unidas para un mundo mejor* (Quito: UNIFEM 1995).

5. See "Hacia la Conferencia Mundial de Mujeres: documento de Venezuela," *Mujeres: una fuerza social en movimiento* (Caracas: JUVECABE, 1995); "Informe del sector no gubernamental," mimeo, Ecuador; "Informe Nacional de las ONGs peruanas," mimeo, Peru; *Plataforma y Coordinadora de la Mujer en Bolivia. Situación de la mujer en Bolivia: 1976-1994. Una protesta con propuesta* (La Paz, 1995); and "Movimiento social de mujeres de Colombia. 1985-1995, mimeo, Colombia.

6. In Ecuador, for example, the Planning and Social Research Centre (CEPLAES)

researched violence and provided services in grassroots neighborhoods in Quito, publishing the *Educational program on husbands' violence against women* in 1992. The Ecuadorian Commission for Cooperation with the Inter-American Women's Commission (CECIM) did research in Guayaquil (1988) to compare violence among grassroots housewives and professional women.

7. Lucila Larrandart, "La mujer en los códigos penales: control sobre el rol de madre," in *La institución policial y los derechos humanos de las mujeres*, p. 55.

8. Facio, "The Principle of Equality Before the Law."

9. Edgar Cordero is a newscast producer with Radio Tomebamba, in Cuenca, Ecuador, which has the largest listenership in the southern highlands, where the population is largely rural and indigenous.

10. For a report on the Ecuador workshops, see Sara Mansilla and Gloria Maira, "Gender and Justice Administration in Ecuador," in Ana Maria Brasileiro, ed., *Building Democracy with Women* (New York: UNIFEM, 1996). See also *Women's Human Rights: Conceptual Approaches.*

Taking Action Against Violence:
A Case Study of Trinidad and Tobago

CECILIA BABB

"... at the heart of the decision to rape, batter and intimidate women (and children) is the ideology of male ownership of women, the many cultural messages in songs and jokes which endorse domestic violence and social conditioning which defines men and women as unequal."

Gender-based violence has emerged as a public political issue in the Caribbean, largely due to the tireless efforts of women's organizations throughout the last two decades. Sustained efforts by women's organizations worldwide have brought about the recognition that violence against women is a crime and a violation of fundamental human rights. For example, at the 1993 World Conference on Human Rights (WCHR) in Vienna, the UN for the first time integrated violence against women and other women's human-rights issues into its general human-rights agenda and activities. Caribbean governments are also ratifying various international conventions such as the Inter-American Convention on the Prevention, Punishment and Eradication of Violence Against Women (Belem Convention) and the Convention on the Elimination of all Forms of Discrimination against Women (CEDAW). They are also signatories to the WCHR Programme of Action and the Declaration and Programme of Action adopted by the Fourth World Conference of Women in Beijing in 1995.

Yet throughout the Caribbean, as throughout the world, violence against women is still most often hidden, making it difficult to observe and measure. Despite general and increasing awareness of its occurrence, it is both trivialized and relegated to the private sphere, where it almost defies intervention. Studies in the region support the widely held theory that the use of violence is essentially a method of controlling women, limiting their freedom of movement, speech and assembly, and undermining their sense of self, their human dignity and their human rights. Its continued invisibility, and increased occurrence, forces women's advocates to rethink the potential of legal approaches in eliminating the problem.

Throughout the region, shifts in the traditional human-rights discourse to embrace an analysis of gender-based violence as a human-rights issue have made possible appeals for state protection of women and the provision of legal remedy for violations to their persons. Domestic violence legislation has been enacted in St. Lucia, St. Vincent and the Grenadines, Jamaica, Trinidad and Tobago, the Bahamas, Grenada, Barbados and Belize, and is currently being considered in Guyana. This legislation gives priority to curtailing a threatened or actual abuse by making protection orders available to the survivor. All of the other Caribbean countries have legislation relevant to domestic violence cases and a few have recently established Family Courts. The Women's Desk of the Caribbean Community (CARICOM) Secretariat has also developed model legislation on domestic violence and sexual offences which governments have drawn on in revising their own legislation. Crisis centres, shelters, legal aid clinics, educational outreach and media watches have also helped survivors of abuse to deal with immediate threats to their safety and integrity.

However, laws have proved inadequate in eliminating, or even drastically curtailing, violence against women, rooted as they are in structural inequality, and the widespread acceptance of this inequality, between men and women. Not the least of their shortcomings has been the insensitivity and opposition of male administrators of the legal process who share an acceptance of gender violence. According to a 1995 CARICOM report, all countries reported an increase in violence against women in the form of physical and sexual assault, including rape, incest, child abuse and neglect. For the year 1993 the number of cases reported ranged from 18 in the Turks and Caicos Islands to 436 in the Bahamas. In Jamaica 92 percent of murder victims in 1994 were women, while sexual violation takes place every eight hours in the Dominican Republic (Clarke 1996).

Although crime rates for Trinidad and Tobago dropped 10 percent between 1991 and 1993 violence against women and children continued to rise (McLeod 1996). Charges of rape, attempted rape and serious indecency rose from 185 to 250 between September and November of 1995, while between January and October of 1994, 23 women were murdered and in the same period for 1995, 12 women and seven children lost their lives to the rage of husbands and fathers. Out of a total of 26 female murders last year, 19 were women and seven were girls; 18 of these victims died as a result of domestic violence. Within a two-week period in 1995, 15 cases of incest were reported (McLeod 1996).

The experience of women's groups and other organizations dealing with violence against women has shown that the problem must be addressed on both an individual level, through long-term counselling for survivors, and at a societal level, by the eradication of inequality between men and women. Solutions must take account of cultural, social and economic factors both at the macro level and at the level of the lives of victims and offenders. This study focuses on the experience of one such group, the Rape Crisis Society of Trinidad and Tobago, in combatting the phenomenon of gender-based violence in the twin island republic of Trinidad and Tobago, situated off the coast of Venezuela.

By the early 1990s, crimes of violence, especially against women and children, had reached unprecedented levels in Trinidad and Tobago. The collapse of the oil sector—the mainstay of the country's economy for the last several decades—in the late 1980s resulted in the embrace of IMF-imposed structural adjustment programmes by successive governments. Combining open markets with cuts in social spending, such programmes have negatively affected the vast majority of the population, resulting in increased poverty and unemployment, and contributing to increase in mental illness, substance abuse, domestic violence, neglect in families and crimes against the person.

While the increase in violence against women must be seen in this context, the phenomenon is by no means new to the republic. It can be traced to the treatment of enslaved women and its perpetuation within family unions throughout emancipation and indentureship to the present. The country's multiethnic population derives from the history of colonization and trade: Spanish, French, and British settlers brought Africans as slaves and Indians and Chinese as indentured workers, whose descendants joined those of traders from Portugal and the Middle East in every possible ethnic combination. Police records and the news media document the incidence for all ethnic groups, social classes and religious affiliations.

The Rape Crisis Society

Although statistics on the incidence of gender-based violence (including sexual harassment) in Trinidad and Tobago were not kept for the period prior to 1985, by 1983, increasingly frequent newspaper reports of rapes and murders of women drew public outrage. For a committed group of men and women, it was not enough to denounce incest and child molestation. It was not enough to sympathize with women who had been raped, physically battered, emotionally abused and terrorized in many ways. In 1984 these individuals formed the Rape Crisis Committee, from which the Rape Crisis Society (RCS) emerged.

The RCS mission is to address issues of sexual violence, particularly as they affect the most vulnerable members of the society. A focal point for active work towards change in all areas affecting these issues, it has become well known for its confidential counselling and support to survivors of gender-based violence, its success in raising public consciousness about all forms of violence (which it unequivocally rejects), and its advocacy and lobbying for legislative reforms that promote gender equality. The RSC also collaborates with agencies and organizations with intersecting interests, such as the police, social units and development agencies.

As the oldest and perhaps only multiethnic organisation intervening specifically in the problem of violence against women in Trinidad and Tobago, the RSC is well respected by the public, the government, the corporate sector and social agencies. It offers counselling to both survivors and offenders, female and male, for acts of violence such as rape, battery, incest, emotional abuse, family problems, kidnapping, and substance abuse. Female survivors from the lower income strata are the most frequent beneficiaries. According to a counsellor, offenders and survivors of higher socio-economic groups fear exposure and tend to seek counselling from practitioners in private practice.

Where Does Violence Come From?

The Rape Crisis Society sees sexual violence as rooted in gender relations, sexuality, family relationships and cultural attitudes. Its members recognize that deteriorating economic conditions serve to exacerbate an already serious problem of sexual violence, as many, especially young men, are unable to cope with the changed gender roles resulting from social and economic pressures and instead turn to violence and drugs to counteract the stress and uncertainty they experience.

Excessive consumption of alcohol, disputes over meals, jealousy, possessiveness, differing expectations about how the role of husband or wife should be performed, and joblessness are all associated with gender-based violence. However, at the heart of the decision to rape, batter and intimidate women (and children) is the ideology of male ownership of women, the many cultural messages in songs and jokes which endorse domestic violence and social conditioning which defines men and women as unequal. Thus sexual and domestic violence must be redefined, not as a private and personal matter about which neighbours and communities say nothing, but as an issue for public discussion and debate. Public debate also allows men to speak, highlighting cultural norms that legitimise male violence as well as enabling them to voice their feelings and concerns about their changing roles.

The removal of domestic violence from the recesses of the home and its exposure to public scrutiny affords communities the opportunity to break the culture of silence and focus on non-violent forms of conflict management and improved self-esteem. The Rape Crisis Society seeks to build awareness that collective action must be based on the realization that while the family is held as sacred, the welfare of individual family members is equally important.

Taking Action Against Violence

From a committed group of 20 in 1984 the Rape Crisis Society has grown to nearly 200 members in 1996.[1] It currently offers annual training for all members, either in counselling survivors or in managing the organization and serving on committees, which include Education, Research and Information Services; Fundraising; Membership and Training.

The organization's first office—The Rape Crisis Centre—was a small room in the Catholic Centre in Port of Spain. A part-time telephone counselling service was gradually extended to a 24-hour hotline service. In response to needs expressed by clients, the RCS also began to provide face-to-face counselling, increasing its caseload from 18 in 1985 to 255 in December 1987. It also embarked on an outreach programme, targeting schools and religious organizations, both to raise public awareness of its existence and to sensitize the public to the issue of sexual violence.

In 1987, with support from the Caribbean Conference of Churches, the Catholic Organization for Development Cooperation, and especially UNIFEM, as well as local fundraising by committee members, the Rape Crisis Centre relocated to a building owned by the Anglican church. By then it was receiving daily requests to conduct educational sessions.

In 1986 the Rape Crisis Society joined other NGOs in demanding that legislation against marital rape be included in the Sexual Offences Act, then being debated in Parliament. After an intense nation-wide public discussion, the act was passed, abolishing the rule of recent complaint, guaranteeing the anonymity of both the complainant and the accused during the course of trial and providing for *in camera* hearings. [2] However, it stipulated that marital rape charges could be brought only in cases where parties have been legally separated. As a result, the RSC decided to undertake greater advocacy campaigns around issues of gender and violence as well as lobbying for more legal reform.

By the end of 1987, the efforts at public education at the community level had encouraged greater reporting of crimes of violence. In 1988 a Rape Crisis Centre was set up in San Fernando in the south of the country, which grew so quickly that it moved to larger premises three years later. By 1988 the hotline service operated 24 hours per day, seven days a week. From 1988 to 1992 some 702 clients received face-to-face counselling and group counselling was successfully introduced. One man from among the husbands with family problems, incestuous fathers, sexual abusers, barterer, homosexuals and the one rapist who attended counselling testified on public radio that "the counselling has helped me to make the change in my life and I have stopped the beating of my wife."

Outreach and networking with other groups intensified along with lobbying for legal reform. In 1991 the Domestic Violence Act was passed. The Rape Crisis Society took on the task of educating both women and men about the application of the Act and its likely impact on family life, targetting workplaces—both public and private agencies—for this activity. The Rape Crisis Centre was also increasingly used as a clearing house of information for state agencies, and as a field placement station for both local and foreign university students.

From its inception the Society has had to draw on the resources of other agencies serving women affected by violence as well as put its services at their disposal in order to maximize its impact on the lives of survivors. Referrals have been made to half-way houses, shelters, social services, police, legal and medical aid agencies. These actions combined with sympathetic and confidential counselling have helped survivors rebuild their shattered lives, regain their self esteem, self respect and dignity. In the words of one survivor, "I no longer hate myself, I am now in love with myself."

The Rape Crisis Society has worked elsewhere in the Caribbean, conducting training for the St. Lucia Crisis Centre and the Guyana Chapter of the Caribbean Association for Feminist Research and Action

(CAFRA). The Society's system for maintaining the confidentiality of cases served as a model for these centres and for the one in Grenada. The RCS also initiated and co-hosted an International/Caribbean Conference on Child Abuse. With CAFRA and the UN Economic Commission for Latin America and the Caribbean it co-hosted a Women, Violence and the Law conference in January 1991.

A Wider View

By the late 1980s the RCS had begun to take a broad developmental approach to gender-based violence. Not content to bandage and salve wounds, the Society targeted that segment of society most guilty of perpetrating violence, men—both to gain insights into their attitudes and behaviour on a range of issues and to jointly arrive at solutions to the situation of violence. Despite years of public education, the incidence of violence was increasing. Also it appeared as if the passage of the Domestic Violence Act had sparked a backlash and men were losing "their cool", as Trinidad and Tobago's Prime Minister put it (Haniff 1996:7).

Following a radio call-in programme, which produced a high rate of male participation, the RSC held a "Men Only Dialogue" workshop in August 1993, which addressed issues of relationships, emotional well-being and communication. A male counsellor also met men in a wide range of situations—as professionals, as students, as unemployed adults, in religious groups, in prison and on the street.

The RSC discovered that men were quite willing to talk about their feelings when their views and opinions were solicited about the roles and expectations society has of them. Many men feel that the system works in favour of women and is hostile to men. They argue that girls receive better treatment at home and school while boys are left to "make up how they could." A 17-year-old feels that: "the girls always top-up", that is, parents always attend to their needs promptly. Men of all ages believe boys are at a great disadvantage in co-educational secondary schools where they compete with girls who are more mature and less easily distracted. Boys attest to "feeling small" because girls do better than them at academic work. Men say that they feel pressured by parents, peers, girl friends and the wider society to have money. They drop out of school to earn money only to find the labour market rife with gender bias favouring women. Meanwhile their sisters are kept in school to continue their education. Men generally express feelings of frustration, helplessness, hopelessness and insecurity.

Many young men have the attitude that through the sex act they are able to display power over women.

In general, however, while men were willing to share their opinions they were not inclined to attend workshops and meetings on a regular basis. Thus the Society conceived the idea of travelling out to rural communities, initiating the "Community Caravan" in March 1995. It makes use of popular theatre, lectures, discussions, film and cultural performances to analyze issues relevant to the community. Ideas, ideals and strategies are collectively proposed and identified for improving family relationships. Between March and September 1995, eight communities were visited, and in four of them, local accommodation has been identified to facilitate continuation of these exercises. Several residents are being trained as lay counsellors and have started using the knowledge gained in their communities. The RCS maintains regular follow-up sessions with these lay counselors.

The Caravan experience showed that communities tend to share the view that it is hopeless to intervene in domestic violence, primarily because women continue in violent relationships. While some people believe that shelters are the answer, these typically offer women and children a safe place for a time during which offenders experience loss of companionship and services. Thus many believe that offenders should be removed to a place where they can be counselled to change their attitude and behaviour. At the same time, they believe communities can organize against violence. It is thought that if perpetrators know that the community will intervene they are likely to think twice before yielding to feelings of anger and power. There is also a call for government to do more to ensure the implementation of progressive legislation.

The experience also showed that men are willing to discuss issues in mixed groups but they are not eager to seek individual counselling, fearing the stigma attached. In general, men are not keen on regular workshops even while they admit that some issues may be more adequately explored in a "Men Only" forum and acknowledge that they feel considerable pressure because of society's expectations. In some communities, however, men have indicated times and places which are convenient for them to participate in the Caravans.

In terms of advocacy, the RSC participated in discussions with other NGOs and made recommendations on two pieces of legislation debated in 1996—the Act to Amend the Constitution and the Act to Amend the

Offences Against the Person Act. In the current review of the Domestic Violence Act 1991, the RCS is again demanding social services to enable women to make use of the Act, such as a family court, foster homes, housing, easier access to government funds for starting income-generating projects, and more shelters. The RCS is also participating, along with other NGOs, in a 24-hour hotline instituted by the Ministry of Culture, Community Development and Women, set up to encourage public discussion and information sharing on the Act. One of the issues being raised is the need for clearer guidelines to police officers about their role in giving meaning to the Act.

The Funding Dilemma

Given its long and extensive experience with issues of gender-based violence and the linkages it has with organizations in Trinidad and Tobago and in the wider Caribbean, the RCS is well placed to spearhead a regional coalition of organizations combating violence. But the Society seems not to be ready for such a role particularly in light of resource scarcity and the subsequent reduction in its activities.

With its success, the RSC has encountered new problems, especially concerning organization and financial self-sufficiency. As the organization grew, a shift from volunteers to paid staff resulted in a serious loss of enthusiasm among the general volunteer membership and it became difficult to retain their interest. The volunteer mode of operating had fostered strong team spirit, emotional gratification and bonds of trust, friendship and interdependence. All activities had been jointly undertaken and success depended on shared resourcefulness and co-operation, creating a shared sense of purpose and risk taking, of pooling of energies, ideas and hopes. The separation of roles and managerial efficiency required by the expanded range of activities, administration of projects and accountability for funds changed the relations among the volunteers.

Growth and expansion called for increased administrative and managerial competence in project implementation and use of funds. The Management Committee focused on developing a strategic plan and mission statement. Clear guidelines were drawn up to direct the operations of the Society, particularly roles and responsibilities of management, volunteers and staff. A Policy and Procedures Manual was also started. Members of the Society were exposed to further training in strategic planning, proposal writing, public speaking and computer literacy.

After RCS self-evaluation in early 1991, the role of the Management Committee was further defined in terms of policy formulation and procurement of funds with attendant supervisory and monitoring functions. During 1992 the Society began to experience problems meeting recurrent expenditure as funding became more and more project specific. In response the Management Committee sought to diversify its funding base, especially in light of UNIFEM's inability to continue extending its support. The government of Trinidad and Tobago began to contribute a monthly subvention in 1993 and new partnerships were initiated with the German government, the Canadian High Commission and the Netherlands.

Income generating projects were more difficult. One project provided counselling to the private sector on the impact of domestic violence on productivity, including absenteeism, sick leave, tardiness and so on, as well as such things as improving team spirit, employee attitude, creativity, inter-personal and inter-departmental functioning. Although welcomed by some sections of the private sector projected revenue failed to materialize. Many workers were uneasy at being identified as having "problems," obliging the RSC rethink its approach.

Other projects were designed to equip survivors with employable skills as well as generate revenue. An agro-processing project and a sewing shop both trained a select number of survivors but did not reach the large number of persons targeted even when special arrangements were made for child care. The projects both floundered when it came to marketing their products.

The Society also doubled its efforts at local fundraising through traditional jumble sales, cake sales, concerts, and curry-ques. Despite its best efforts to do much work with little money, its ingenuity in obtaining labour, materials and services, its ability to attract significant external funding, money has never been enough to respond to demands and to carry out needed activities. Staff had to be reduced, increasing workloads and depressing morale. Low salaries meant that trained employees moved on, taking with them valuable work experience. Increased reliance on volunteers has not been an entirely satisfactory alternative since many members either lack the necessary skills or cannot sustain their voluntary services for a variety of personal reasons. The Society has had to continuously train new counsellors to meet its needs. Financial stress has also prevented long-range planning.

Lessons Learned

More than a decade of intervention into gender-based violence has yielded in-depth knowledge about the nature and extent of the problem as well as an understanding of the organizational development and institutional competence needed to intervene efficiently. The most disturbing realization is that violence against women, far from decreasing, continues to escalate, despite the passage of legislation aimed at effecting gender equality. While hard data is not available, anecdotal evidence and media reports all attest to an alarming increase in the spate of violent acts against women. The following lessons can be drawn:

First, and most important, intervention can only succeed if incidences of violence are reduced. Counselling of survivors must go hand in hand with counselling of abusers, who must be persuaded to change their behaviour and tolerate gender equality in their relationships, and also spread that message to other men.[3] Other educational and socialising agents also have a role in violence prevention. Teachers and social workers must be sensitised to recognize child abuse and trained in the management of conflict on the playing field, on the streets, in groups and other situations where differences and tensions arise. The media must engage in efforts to reduce and prevent violence to women, promoting the belief that all forms of violence are wrong and condemning images which promote the objectification of people and glorify violence. The churches must help to assist families to manage feelings which hurt their members.

Second, progress in the ideological relations of gender reflected in legislation such as the Sexual Offences Act and the Domestic Violence Act must be buttressed by actions in the material sphere if survivors are to be emotionally and financially empowered. Clearly, there must be adequate state provided shelters at which women can be safe and children accommodated while offenders are rehabilitated. Where necessary counselling has to be reinforced by the provision of life and work skills to reduce feelings of dependence and helplessness. Medical and legal services must also be available. Since the entire family is affected when abuse takes place in the home, provision must be made for counselling children so that they can deal with the trauma.

Third, despite the need to be self sufficient, an agency set up to provide emotional support to survivors of violence cannot easily embark on business ventures, which themselves call for special expertise and particular resources. In the same way that the Society has had to set up centres as its operational units, so too a separate entity will have to be set up to generate income to finance the centres' work.

Fourth, careful screening of potential trainees in order to assess their commitment to serving as counsellors is critical. The Centre's obligation to survivors requires it to use its resources to make more counsellors available to it, not simply to expose interested persons to counselling techniques.

Fifth, extensive dependence on volunteers does not necessarily reduce the need for a lot of money to operate centres. In fact, the presence of volunteers sometimes spurs an agency to take on more and more functions, without paying due attention to the real costs of the projects. Volunteers must have certain skills besides interest in the issue of violence to women. Enthusiasm goes a long way in putting to use academic excellence and experience that might not otherwise have been tapped, but practical skills are also needed, especially skills in negotiating, accessing and managing financial resources.

Sixth, each component of a programme should be treated as a discrete project for the purposes of fundraising and allocating expenditure. Severe mismanagement problems can arise when one risks juggling funds between projects in order to keep them afloat.

Seventh, and even more sobering, paid staff should not be expected to work as hard as the core of volunteers who started the programme. While those who started the Society would have given more of themselves, paid staff should not be expected to demonstrate similar levels of commitment and sacrifice.

Violence Against Women: Obstacle to Development

While the incidence of abuse cuts across all social classes and ages, two studies on family violence commissioned by CARICOM for the International Year of the Family showed that more cases of abuse are reported for women in the lower socio-economic strata. A study on women's reproductive health, conducted in 1995 by the Institute of Social and Economic Research in Jamaica and Barbados identifies the family as the primary location of violence, while a CARICOM study found that the greatest threat of violence to women comes from their families and partners; in 1995, most women seeking shelter in Trinidad and Tobago, for example, were housewives (Mondesire and Dunn 1995; Clarke 1995).

Violence against women also crosses racial lines. Even so, the CARICOM study noted that some 80 percent of women seeking shelter in

Trinidad and Tobago were East Indian. Haniff (1996) records that when the Domestic Violence Act, 1991 was passed there was a spate of wife killings, many of them East Indian women. Prime Minister Panday is quoted as saying that these violent incidents stemmed from the restraining orders granted under the Act. A psychiatrist stated that "women were not behaving in the best interest of the families" in seeking restraining orders and were therefore provoking violent responses from men (Haniff 1996). The sons and brothers of women who are murdered feel sympathy for the men who kill, understand their dilemma and try to explain away their motivations.

A large proportion of homicides by East Indian men in Trinidad have been perpetrated against their wives, lovers and children. In many cases women were killed because they wanted to be separate. This rejection is such a blow to a man's public self, so critical to his definition of manhood, that the woman cannot continue to live unless she remains with him. Poynting (1981), Reddock (1988) and more recently Mohammed (1996), noting the many murders of East Indian women by their partners in the late 19th century and early 20th century, explain the phenomenon as a manifestation of male refusal to accept women's efforts to define their lives on their own terms, indicating an underlying fear of loss of gender identity and power which is central to Indian masculinity.[4] Haniff (1966) sees violence within the East Indian family as a strong male reaction to any crisis centered around definitions of male and female.

However, while spousal murders are not as common among Afro Trinidadian women, their abuse is as widespread. Beckles (1996) points to the role of slavery in alienating fatherhood and focusing its attention on motherhood. He also highlights the systems of violent terror used to suppress any insubordination. However, Michael Flood (1996) gets to the heart of the matter, arguing that it is the socially produced ideal of hegemonic masculinity which burdens the relations between men and women, lacing them with violence.

In the Caribbean convictions for crimes of violence against women are disturbingly low, numbering 15 out of 702 domestic violence cases in St. Vincent and the Grenadines in 1994, and 115 out of 323 cases of sexual assault in Jamaica. Between April 1991 and April 1994 in excess of 8,000 cases of domestic violence had accumulated for hearing in the Magistrates Courts of Trinidad and Tobago (Clarke 1996; Mondesire and Dunn, 1995).

Perhaps the greatest challenge to addressing problems of domestic violence in Trinidad and Tobago is the perception by many that it is not a crime. Indeed some children in school have argued that women who fail to cook for their husbands "deserve a good lash" and that women who wear revealing clothes or who go out at nights to parties are asking to be raped.

For reasons ranging from emotional and economic dependence, to the belief that it is the responsibility of a woman to make relationships work, women remain in abusive situations. The tendency to self-blame allows women who have been raped to feel responsible for their offenders' actions, especially when the perpetrator is an acquaintance.

In ordinary incidences of assault the victim's only contact with an offender is usually at the time that the offense was committed and during the trial. A woman who lives out her days in the same space as her attacker, terrified, trying not to bring on another attack and grateful for any acts of kindness must lose her sense of self. Women who live with verbal abuse and humiliation over extended periods cannot retain their self-esteem and self-confidence. A woman who lives with the memory of rape must necessarily disassociate herself from her body in order to go on living. The offender who thrives on such dismal power must lose his humanity if these acts are repeated often enough.

Violence as the embodiment of masculinity must be erased. Wars and executions must stop. Violence as the theme of jokes, songs and movies must be stopped. Violence as a demonstration of might and power must be stopped. Violence against women impairs their enjoyment of their fundamental rights to security and happiness, destroys their health and productive capacity while incurring both medical and legal expenditure to the state, is an obstacle to development and a blot on civilization.   ❖

Notes

1. The original 20, both men and women, participated in a training programme conducted by the director of the Rape Crisis Programme of St. Vincent's Hospital in New York City, which included the social, economic and psychological aspects of rape, the medical and legal aspects of sexual crimes, and training in face to face and telephone counselling.

2. The provision means that survivors of violent acts would no longer be penalised for delayed reporting.

3. The RSC seeks funds to launch Male Support Groups for partners of survivors of sexual abuse, batterers, violent males and men with family problems.

4. In Trinidad and Tobago between 1859 and 1863, there were 27 wife murders. In British Guiana between 1894-1905 there were 29 murders of Indian women.

References

Barbados Report on the Society for International Development National Day of Reflection. November 1994.

Beckles, Hilary (1996). "Black Masculinity in Caribbean Slavery," WAND Occasional Paper, February 1996.

CAFRA (1991). *Report on the Regional Meeting on Women, Violence and the Law.* Trinidad and Tobago: CAFRA.

_____(n.d.). *Domestic Violence and the Law.*

Carrillo, Roxanna (1992). *Battered Dreams: Violence Against Women as an Obstacle to Development.* New York: UNIFEM.

Clarke, Roberta (1996). "Violence Against Women in the Caribbean: State and Non-State Responses." Jamaica: UNIFEM.

_____ 1995. "Violence Against Women: The Usefulness of the Human Rights Discourse." Jamaica: UNIFEM.

Engle, Patrice (1994). *Men in Families: Report of a Consultation on the Role of Males and Fathers in Achieving Gender Equality.* New York: UNICEF.

Flood, Michael (1966). "Heterosexual Men and Sexuality". WAND Occasional Paper 4/96.

Haniff, Nesha (1966). "The Stereotyping of East Indian Women in the Caribbean," WAND Occasional Paper, January 1996.

Henry, Ralph and Norma Demas (1991). "A Situational Analysis of Women and Children in Trinidad and Tobago in 1990." Trinidad and Tobago: UNICEF.

McLeod, Michelle I. (1996). "Thin Line Between Love and Hate: A Reality, Not a Thriller," *Trinidad Guardian,* May 27, 1996.

Mohammed, Patricia (1996). "The Negotiation of Gender Relations and Identity Among Indians in Village Trinidad in the Post-Indentureship Period," WAND Occasional Paper, February 1996.

Mondesire, Alicia and Alicia Dunn (1995). *Towards Equity in Development: A Report on the Status of Women in Sixteen Commonwealth Caribbean Countries.* Georgetown: CARICOM.

Stuart, Sheila (1996). "Gender and Reproductive Health in the Caribbean." ISER Seminar Series No. 3.

Notes on Contributors

Gladys Acosta Vargas is a feminist lawyer and consultant on women's human rights for several UN agencies, including UNICEF and UNIFEM. A former director of the Flora Tristán Centre in Lima, Peru she was co-ordinator of the Gender and Power Programme in Bogotá, Colombia from 1992 to 1996. She is the author of numerous articles on women's human rights, legislative reform and judicial theory.

Cecilia Babb, a national of Dominica and Barbados, is programme officer for the Caribbean NGO Policy Development Centre in Barbados. She has done extensive research on women and development in the Caribbean, including the impact of structural adjustment on women and women's reproductive health.

Roxanna Carrillo directs the Women's Human Rights Programme at UNIFEM and manages the Trust Fund in Support of Actions to Eliminate Violence Against Women. A co-founder of the Flora Tristán Centre in Peru and the U.S.-based Centre for Women's Global Leadership, she is the author of numerous books and articles on violence against women and women's human rights.

Roberta Clarke is a practising attorney based in Trinidad and Tobago. Since 1989, she has worked as Project Co-ordinator for the Caribbean Association for Feminist Research and Action on its Women and the Law and Gender and Human Rights programmes. She is curently Vice Chair of the Board of Women, Law and Development International, based in Washington, DC.

Patricia Duarte Sánchez, a biologist, is co-founder and director of the Mexican Collective to Fight Violence Against Women (COVAC). She has been working with women who have been victims of violence since 1980 and is the author of several books and articles on this topic.

Gerardo González, a lawyer, is co-founder of the Mexican Collective to Fight Violence Against Women (COVAC), for which he is now an advisor. A professor of law at the Autonomous Metropolitican University in Mexico City, he is the author of several books and articles on gender violence.

Alexandra Ayala Marín, a feminist journalist, is publisher and editor of Fempress Magazine, in Quito, Ecuador.

Marcela Ortiz is a Chilean journalist who has worked on newspapers and journals in Algeria and Mexico as well as Chile. Since 1993, she has worked for ISIS International in Chile, where she currently edits its Bulletin of the Violence Against Women Programme and, during 1995 edited its newsletter, *Hacia Beijing*.

Heleith I.B. Saffioti is a sociologist and Professor of Social Sciences at the Catholic University of São Paulo in Brazil. She is the author of numerous books and articles on women, gender and development and women's human rights.

Virginia Vargas, a feminist sociologist and activist, was Co-founder of the Flora Tristán Centre in Peru and was Latin American and Caribbean co-ordinator for participation in the Fourth World Conference on Women in Beijing in 1995. She is the author of numerous books and articles on issues of women and development.